Memoir of a Cashier

Korean Americans, Racism, and Riots

Carol Park

Image 5 & 6 by Hyungwon Kang.

ISBN: 978-0-9982-9570-1 (sc)
ISBN: 978-0-9982-9571-8 (hc)
ISBN: 978-0-9982-9572-5 (e)

Library of Congress Control Number: 2017900590

The Young Oak Kim Center for Korean American Studies
at the University of California Riverside
4031 CHASS INTN, Riverside, CA, 92521
951-827-5661
The Young Oak Kim Center for Korean American Studies
at the University of California Riverside

rev. date: 01/30/2017

For Mom, Albert, and Tony

Acknowledgements

Family is everything to me, and I want to thank mine for their love and support. We have been through so much together, and yet none of the hardships have broken our bond. Mom is the reason my family is still together. Her strength and perseverance after Dad died is inspiring. Even when she suffered through countless difficulties, endured marathon shifts at work, and had no one to help her raise three young children, she carried on and provided for her family; there are no words of gratitude that can describe how much I appreciate what she did. She is the definition of a strong woman and mother.

Also, a sincere thank you to Professor Edward T. Chang for his guidance, belief, and support in this project. I am indebted to him for his encouragement. I am grateful to him for all that he does for the Korean American community.

The inspiration for this project began in 2009 during a class I was enrolled in as part of the Master of Fine Arts in Creative Writing at the University of California Riverside, Palm Desert Low Residency Program. I was in a class with author Deanne Stillman. She saw the very first pages of this book, and it is because of her encouragement that I followed through on this endeavor.

This book has been through several drafts, and were it not for the constant reassurance of my best friend Massiel Ladron De Guevara, I would have sat down and cried long ago. I was only able to complete this project because of the support of family, close friends, teachers, and mentors. Thank you to all the people that have helped me on this journey.

Foreword

This book introduces an emerging voice in the field of Korean American Studies. This mesmerizing tale of a Korean American girl living a dual life as a cashier and obedient daughter is captivating in its directness and honesty. From witnessing shootings, enduring relentless racism, dealing with the Black-Korean Conflict of the 1980s and 1990s, and fearing for her safety, the author's visceral illustration of her world is fascinating. Most importantly, in the chapter that deals with the 1992 LA Riots – or *Sa-i-gu* as Koreans call it – she paints a harrowing scene of anxiety, anguish, and sadness that captures the Korean American experience at that time.

I have known the author for several years. She is an efficient and intelligent researcher whose passion involves bridging the cultural gaps between Korean Americans and other ethnicities. She creatively connects her personal life with her work life and weaves in the Korean American story expertly. She is open about her personal struggle with racism and anger and how she overcame those obstacles. This book represents her goal of raising the Korean American voice and identity within the national narrative.

But before delving further into this story, it's important to understand the Korean American journey and why and how Koreans ended up in America, and how they have grown, struggled, and survived. Korean American history is a tale filled with hardships, accomplishments, tragedies, and joy. In the late 1800s, a small number of Koreans travelled to the United States as ginseng merchants, selling their herbs to Chinese railroad workers. Official Korean immigration to the United States began on January 13, 1903 after the Hawaiian Sugar Plantation Association (HSPA) encouraged the importation of a new labor force. The *S. S. Gaelic* sailed to the United States with 102 Koreans and landed in Honolulu,

Hawaii. The Koreans were welcomed by the HSPA and put to work on sugar plantations. By 1905, the Hawaiian plantations were home to 7,226 Koreans. Today, we celebrate January 13 as Korean American Day.

Well-known Koreans, including Philip Jaisohn (Soh Jaipil), Dosan Ahn Chang Ho, and Syngman Rhee, lived and worked in the United States in the late 1800s and early 1900s. In fact, Jaisohn was the first Korean to become a naturalized U.S. citizen in 1890. He later became the first Korean to earn a medical degree in the United States.

In 1905, Dosan founded the first organized Korean American settlement (Koreatown) at Pachappa Camp in Riverside, CA. He helped the Riverside community thrive and mobilized Koreans there to work for the independence of Korea. Meanwhile, Koreans established the Riverside chapter of the Korean National Association (KNA) in the Pachappa community. In 1911, the annual meeting of the KNA was held at the site; the gathering was hailed as the most successful KNA meeting at the time as all the chapter presidents – excluding Mexico's delegate – attended the two-week conference.

In the early 1900s, many Koreans lived all over California in places like Riverside, Redlands, Upland, and Claremont. They had moved throughout the nation, in states like New Jersey and Missouri. Koreans worked hard as farm laborers and focused on supporting independence activities. In 1920, a group of Koreans founded the Willows Korean Aviation School Corps in Willows, CA. The school trained fighter pilots for the Korean independence movement. Kim Chong Lim, the first Korean American millionaire, and Korean Provisional Government General Ro Paik Lin were instrumental in the school's funding and direction.

By the 1930s, Korean Americans were living and working in large city centers like Los Angeles. When World War II broke out in 1939, Koreans enlisted in the U.S. Army or were drafted. One of those brave Korean Americans was Col. Young Oak Kim (1919-2005). He helped lead the famous Nisei unit the 100th Battalion, and fought in Italy, France, and Germany. He earned the equivalent of the Medal of Honor from Italy, Korea, and France. (Yet he still has not received the honor from his birth-country, the United States.) Kim became a humanitarian after he retired from the military, and his work continues to echo in our community today.

By the 1940s and 1950s, another Korean American made history by becoming the first Asian American to win gold for the United States. Dr. Sammy Lee won a gold medal for diving in the 1948 and 1952 Olympic Games. Koreans, who were still a small and little-known minority in the United States, became a household name when the Korean War broke out in 1950. For three years, the war raged on until an armistice agreement was signed and a ceasefire was put in place. But, with fighting quelled and interest subdued, Korean Americans again became a forgotten community. However, by the 1960s and 1970s, with the passage of the 1965 Immigration and Nationality Act, more Koreans could migrate to the United States, and the Korean American population began to increase.

Much like the first Koreans to arrive in America, this new wave of Korean immigrants was faced with discrimination and poor job opportunities. Korean Americans were forced to find other means of survival and turned to small business. With little money or help, Koreans looked to open businesses in inner cities like Compton, California, Chicago, and Flushing, New York. By the 1980s, Korean Americans were once again in the American media spotlight, this time as rude business owners who were often involved in shootings with the black community. The problem was known as the Black-Korean Conflict and was exacerbated by the American press.

Korean shops, located in poor and underserved inner cities, were blamed for the racial tension. By 1992, after the not-guilty verdict in the Rodney King beating case, the tension exploded. Rioting and looting occurred as the African-American community protested the verdicts. Koreans became the target of looters and rioters as buildings were destroyed and businesses were ransacked.

After the six days of rioting, the birth or re-birth of the Korean American identity occurred. The wake-up call made Korean Americans realize they needed to communicate with the communities their businesses were part of, participate in politics, and raise their voices. After the LA Riots, the Korean American community became stronger with a visible identity.

Today, the Korean American population is spread throughout the United States. The US Census Bureau estimated the total Korean American population at more than 1.8 million in 2012. The highest concentration of Koreans resides in Los Angeles County, California where the population reached 217,260 in 2014.[1] Symbolically, the heart of the Korean American community is in Los Angeles in an ethnic enclave known as Koreatown. The popularity of Koreans soared in the early 2000s with the Hallyu Wave, as Korean culture and food hit mainstream American society hard. Bulgogi tacos, kimchi, and Korean barbeque, Korean dramas and music, and even Korean American actors took the American pop-culture scene by surprise.

But this book is more than just part of the Hallyu Wave; it is a story that we can all relate to.

Edward T. Chang
Prof. of Ethnic Studies, UC Riverside
Director, YOK Center, UC Riverside
Riverside, November 2016

Preface

This project has been years in the making, and without the proper guidance, support, and faith of my family, teachers, and friends, I would still be twiddling my thumbs. This book is a work of creative nonfiction. Scenes have been reconstructed from memory, interviews, and research. I've changed several names of non-public figures to protect their identities. Most the scenes are a mix of events that occurred in my life from age ten to eighteen.

After growing up watching media fan the flames of ethnic strife in the 1980s and 1990s, pitting one minority against the other, I sought to give voice to the Korean American community. At the time of the 1992 LA Riots, I was too young to do anything. But years later, when I was old enough, I became a journalist for one of the local Inland Empire, California papers, and later, I wrote for various newspapers, magazines, and journals. For several years, I learned my craft: how to cover a story, hit deadlines, and become a better writer. The skills I obtained as a journalist – interviewing, researching, writing – gave me the tools I needed to compose this book.

When I began this project, it was a cathartic exercise. But as the words flowed, I realized I needed to tell this tale of not just my family, but of many Korean Americans who suffered through the 1992 Los Angeles Riots, endured racism, and were pigeonholed into the model-minority stereotype.

The Korean American voice was not heard during those tumultuous years leading up to the LA Riots. Even during, and for some time after the riots, Korean Americans had little representation. Often, it is said that the LA Riots were a turning point for Korean American identity, which was born or re-born during that time. For me, the LA Riots represent a watershed moment that opened my eyes.

While the visibility of Korean Americans has grown with the popularity of Korean food, K-pop, and K-drama, the socio-economic conditions that helped to incite the LA Riots are still issues faced today. Police brutality, poverty, racism, and lack of education are just a few of the many ingredients that boiled over in a froth of violence on *Sa-i-gu*. In the last few years there have been riots, uprisings, and civil unrests in places like Baltimore, Maryland and Ferguson, Missouri. Not much has changed since April 29, 1992.

This book is meant to provide a bird's-eye view into my Korean American life. That view is offered up in the story of how my world changed and was affected by the things I witnessed while working in that tiny, bulletproof cashier's booth at Mom's gas station in Compton in the 1990s.

After years of work, some tears, and help from friends and mentors, this book is finally complete. It is my hope that this work of creative nonfiction will help provide a better understanding of the Korean American journey.

Chapter 1

Throwback Thursday

"Sir, if you're going to be racist, please, get it right," I said one late evening in the early 1990s. "I'm not a chink or a Jap. I'm Korean. You can call me a gook."

The tall black man glowered at me as I stared back at him, our eyes locked in racial warfare that started between our two ethnicities in the late 1970s and early 1980s. I was working a shift with Mom at her gas station in Compton, California.

"Bitch," the man said.

"Fuck you," I yelled as he walked away.

This was the memory that flashed through my mind when news of the Baltimore, Maryland Riots of April 2015 made headlines. Rioters, looters, protesters, random bystanders, and pretty much everyone and their mother were all jumbled up in a mix of violence and outcry at the death of Freddie Gray. Police brutality was once again the alleged culprit in the young black man's death. I followed the coverage of the riots. *Why haven't things changed? Will they ever change?* I thought.

Fires burned in Baltimore and businesses were torched – businesses owned by Koreans and other minorities, people like my mom. My thoughts reached back to the 1992 Los Angeles Riots, when I was just a child learning about the finer details of life. Twenty-three years before the Baltimore Riots, the not-guilty verdict in the Rodney King beating case sent Los Angeles into a whirlwind of chaos. At the time of the LA Riots, I was working weekend shifts with Mom at the gas station. I hated every second I spent in that small bulletproof cashier's booth. It took years for me to find myself, my voice, and the strength to overcome the racism and hate I had harbored from the hours, days, and years I worked at that gas station. Nevertheless, that booth was my classroom; it was the place that taught me why and how the Baltimore Riots were just a repeat of the same damn thing.

I clicked through slideshow images of police officers and protestors clashing in the streets of Baltimore. For a moment, I was back in Compton with Mom. I shook my head in dismay and decided to call her.

"Did you see what's happening in Baltimore?" I asked her in Korean. We almost always speak to each other in Korean.

"Yes."

"What do you think?"

"Same thing," she said. "There's no difference."

"It's sad," I said. "Did you see that Korean store owners lost a lot?"

She was quiet.

"Mom?"

"Don't worry yourself about these things," she said. "You don't have to anymore."

But she was wrong. I did have to worry. After all, I dedicated my career to understanding this kind of stuff. My job as a Korean American Studies researcher demanded that I be concerned, that I care, and that I be more than just the daughter of an immigrant living the "American Dream."

During the 2015 Baltimore Riots, 380 businesses were looted or damaged; about 100 were owned by Korean Americans.[2] In the 1992 LA Riots, more than 2,200 Korean American stores were looted, burned, or damaged.[3] The difference this time around in terms of what sparked the violence – excluding the numbers – is not very much. Koreans are more visible in American culture than they were twenty-five years ago, but the structural conditions that ignited the LA Riots still exist today.

"Mom, I am worried," I said. "You never know when this is going to happen again, whether in Baltimore or LA, or anywhere else."

"Stop wasting your time," she said. "Go back to work."

She hung up.

Mom's a strong Korean woman. She doesn't mince words with anyone. She's hard-working. She's determined to give me and my two older brothers – Tony and Albert – a better life than she had, growing up on a farm in a shack stuffed with nine people and not enough food or clothes to keep anyone full or warm. So, why would she worry herself about something like the Baltimore Riots when she'd already gone through something like that in 1992? She'd done her job and raised her children to be happy and successful, but she never considered the fact that the images of the Baltimore unrest would stir up resentment, bitterness, and anger in me. My mind raced back to the first time I went to the gas station, the first time I realized I am more than just an American, I am an immigrant's daughter, born to carry the burden of a dual-identity and all the shitty, beautiful things that come with it…

"Carol, get up," Mom said to me one Saturday morning. "Get dressed."

I gathered my consciousness and looked at her standing in the bedroom doorway. She was dressed in her black pants and black cardigan. She always wore black. Ever since Dad died, it was like black was her new favorite color. I got up without saying a word, and she went downstairs. I went to my closet and pulled aside the big mirror door, a remnant from the 1970s décor the house came with. I dug through my pile of clothes and found my favorite jeans. I pulled a dark blue sweater over my head. Mom yelled at me to hurry up, we were going to be late. I nearly tripped over myself running down the stairs. Mom held the giant oak door open for me as I hustled my tired limbs out to the car with her. She drove us to the gas station. The fluorescent lights lit up the twelve-pump property like it was Christmas morning. I followed her into the cashier's booth. I looked around and rubbed the sleep out of my eyes. The worker we were changing shifts with said hello. He was a nice man that would later become the pastor of a church I attended as a teenager. Mom opened the new shift and the worker left.

"Come over here," she said.

I had been standing by the doorway watching the worker and Mom go about their business. I walked over to where she was standing. There was a plastic crate; Mom grabbed it and set it next to the cash register.

"Oh look," she said. "You're double digits now. You can work."

She told me to stand on the box so I could see better. I didn't need it; I was tall for a ten-year-old. But Mom wanted me to get a clear picture of the cashbox. I looked at the colors of the keys – blue, white, green, black, and red – and gave her a puzzled look. What the heck was I supposed to do? Mom pointed at the numbered buttons; the black shapes stood out against the white of the keys; they reminded me of the piano we had at home in the living room. Mom proceeded to teach me how to turn on the pumps, how to give change, and correct mistakes.

"Don't ever press this red one, not unless there's an emergency," she finally said as she pointed to a large, red, angry-looking button with the word "STOP" boldly printed in white. My brain imagined what the hell an emergency would be. I thought about cars blowing up and bursting into flames. I thought about people crashing their vehicles into the pumps. I imagined accidents and bloodied drivers staggering about the streets. I thought about gun battles and other random things I'd seen on television.

"Okay?" Mom asked.

I looked at her, the reverie of emergency situations still fresh in my mind, and nodded. I stayed with her in the booth for hours taking my first class in Cashiering 101. She let me punch in the numbers as customers came and left. She chided me when I made mistakes. Hours ticked by, and before I realized it, the sun had peaked to high noon.

So began my illustrious career as a gas station cashier.

At some point, I asked Mom for a uniform. I wanted the sky-blue mechanic's shirt Dad used to wear. Mom walked over to a drawer in her room one morning and pulled out a short-sleeved shirt. It was a button-up and had an orange, blue, and white name patch with dad's name – Tony Sr. – sewn on the top right; it also had a pocket on the left.

"Wear this," she said. "It was your dad's."

The next shift we worked, I wore the uniform over a black long-sleeve. It was baggy, but I felt like a real employee. I was ready to refine and polish my craft. In the first year of my new job as daughter-laborer – 1990 – I learned a lot. I picked up street lingo and cuss words I never knew existed: "whore," "dog-shit-eating bitch," and so on. I also learned about even more wonderful things like racism. I learned that people saw me as a chink, nip, Jap, oriental, gook, yellow-skinned whore, FOB, and slanted-eye "insert derogatory adjective here." I didn't quite understand it at the time, this thing called racism and that thing called discrimination. I grew up an American. So, when I started getting called racist names, I got mad.

"Fuck you" became a daily, even hourly phrase I used. "Fuck you" became a mantra. "Fuck you" became a weapon. As I got my street education while working shifts and watching people, I picked up racist words I could use, things like the "n" word and other unsavory names. My life as a cashier was anything but joyful. This bulletproof box I lived, breathed, and feared in was a place I hated. But at least I was never bored.

My life before the cashier's booth was chaotic in its own way. On May 5, 1990, Dad died from cirrhosis of the liver. He was an avid drinker and smoker. He was also an ambitious man, and by 1989 he had amassed a cache of gas stations – five in all. The first one he bought was on Figueroa Street in Los Angeles; he later sold it. Then in 1974, he bought the one in Compton and eventually three in Long Beach, and another in Lakewood. People in the area called him Tony. Mom was simply "Mrs. Park." No one ever called her by her first name: Son. I'd like to think it's because they respected her.

When Dad was alive, Mom learned the ropes of the business from observation. She made sure to understand how to order gas, fix a pump, and run a shift. She learned how to manage a mechanic's bay. The station she inherited from Dad was large; it had twelve pumps and occupied one corner of the intersection of Rosecrans and Atlantic Avenues. The station also housed a three-car garage bay.

The inside of the cashier's booth was small. Metal countertops served as anchors for the inventory of candy, soda, flavored cigars, peanuts, and cough drops. Cigarettes were stacked ten to a row across the rear wall that separated the booth from the back office. The exterior of the cashier's booth was enclosed with bulletproof glass windows and solid gray rock at the bottom. The word "CASHIER" and a big arrow were painted in red above the bulletproof glass windows that made up the booth. The building was made of metal sheets.

The cashier's booth with the big red lettering and arrow. The booth had two sides for customers to pay: one facing Atlantic Avenue, the other facing Rosecrans. (Photo from family archives).

Mom knew every inch of the station, and she cultivated all the little things necessary to operate it. As a Korean woman, wife, and mother, she did all of this without any hesitation or thought for herself. Korean women like Mom were raised to be hardworking and to sacrifice themselves for the well-being of their families. The same was expected of me. So, that's what I did, I worked at that gas station with the flickering light in the corner that reminded me every night that life is no ball. Even when I was old enough to say enough-is-enough, I still worked with Mom because that's just what you do when your dad is dead and you and your family are left to work 48-hour shifts without batting a damn fucking eye... that's just what you do.

On that first day of Cashiering 101, I had no idea what I was getting into nor did I know anything about the chaotic history of the city of Compton or anything about the Black-Korean Conflict overall. I had no idea that my slanted eyes were a source of hostility in the racially divided inner cities of the United States. Koreans and blacks didn't get along. Mexicans and blacks didn't get along. Koreans and other Asian ethnic groups got along with whites because we were a so-called model minority.[4] Don't even get me started on the black-white conflict. This is the setting of my childhood. This is the melting pot of violence and discrimination I was thrust into as a ten-year-old. But let me not digress.

The gas station; twelve pumps total. Location, Rosecrans and Atlantic Avenues in Compton, CA. (Photo from family archives).

Mom in the booth on a busy afternoon in 2012.
Photo by Keun-pyo "Root" Park.

Chapter 2

Journey to the Dark Side

The night was young, and I was standing in the cashier's booth for the umpteenth time in a row. I stared at the gum, candy, and soda we were selling to supplement our gas sales. Thank goodness we didn't sell alcohol like they did at the rival station across the street. They were constantly being robbed. At least once a week someone would run in and shoplift 24-packs of beer. They had a snack shop you could walk into, we didn't. (At least not until it was the late 1990s and even then, we kept the cashbox behind bulletproof glass).

Mom was dozing in the back office. I was sitting on my blue cushioned seat; it fit snuggly between the register and the wall. I drummed my fingers on the metal countertop and thought about how many times I'd been called a racial slur that month. The weekend before, someone called me a "chink, nip, whore of a bitch." I mean, the creativity and thought these assholes put into their insults amazed me. Every weekend for months someone would say something like that to me. At first it was shocking, but after a while, I got over it and started cussing right back. After all, one good turn deserves another, right?

"Everything okay, Carol?" Mom asked as she walked into the booth a few moments later. "Did you fight with one of the customers again?"

"I got called a chink. Why does that keep happening?"

She brushed some of her permed hair out of her face. I could see some grey in her once jet black curls. She straightened some of the boxes of candies we had laid out on the countertops in front of the windows. I followed her gaze as she did a once-over of the station.

"Just be nice," she finally said. "Don't worry about what people call you. Just be nice."

"No way," I said. "They don't care, so why should I?"

Mom left me to my own devices and went back to the office. The hours ticked by. Customers that came to the window didn't look twice at me and never questioned the fact that I was just a kid working a graveyard shift. They'd seen Koreans putting their kids to work at other places like liquor stores and wig shops. Seeing me there was no big surprise for folks in the area. Koreans like Mom put their kids to work so they could not only learn the value of a dollar, but also out of necessity.

"Damn gooks!" a black man who had just asked for five bucks of gas said as he walked up to the booth. "Make that shit go faster! Look at how slow it's goin'. You little nip, don't you be tryin' to rip me off!"

I was tired. I was hungry. I was annoyed. I was getting angry. I tried to ignore him.

"You listenin' to me?"

He hit the metal tray. He yelled at me and kept cussing; cursing over and over. His tirade was relentless.

"Shitty Koreans!" he said. "Comin' up in the hood, overchargin' us, taking our jobs!"

"Hey asshole, get the hell out of here!" I finally said. "I'll call the cops!"

"Dirty, greedy Korean," he said. "Screw you and your chink-ass family."

I tried to keep my temper. But how many times had someone yelled at me like this? How many times had I been called a "gook," a "chink," a "nip," and cussed at for no good reason? How many times had I just stood there and taken it? How many damn times had I just been nice like mom told me to be? How many freaking times?!

"You dumb [n-word]," I finally said as I stared at him. "What's wrong with you?! The pump is working! Stop yelling!"

He glowered at me. He was furious. He balled his hand into a fist. I got scared. I had just called someone the "n" word for the first time in my life; something I knew I should never do, but I had done it because I was so tired of being cussed at. I was tired of being blamed for something I had no control over.

"What did you just say?" he said as he cocked his head to the left. "What did you just call me?"

"I'm not trying to rip you off," I said calmly. "Stop cussing at me. Go away."

"You best watch what the hell you say, kid," he said as he pointed a finger at me. "If you know what's good for you, watch what the fuck you say."

I turned away from him. He stood there for a few more seconds staring at me before he finally walked off. I sat down on my blue-cushioned seat and let out a sigh of relief. I had just crossed the line.

Some would call this moment the beginning of my journey to the dark side. I hated the bulletproof box I worked in. I hated most of the customers. I couldn't stand looking at the cigarettes that were stacked ten to a row in vertical slats on the wall above my chair. The multiple colors of red, green, blue, and gold were like a rainbow of joy that didn't belong over my head. I despised the candies we sold – I was so sick of eating them. Even the way the booth was laid out annoyed me: the two windows made it difficult to handle a lot of customers at once. No one had patience, and no one cared. The rage spilled over into my daily life and changed me in ways that would make even the emperor proud.

Mom, however, was a different story. She did her best to be "nice," as she always told me to be. She was always very conscientious about her word choices. She was considerate and kind to customers, cutting them breaks on car repairs, and giving loans to workers who asked for it and hiring mechanics based off recommendations from people in the surrounding neighborhood. But that doesn't mean she was one hundred percent perfect. Oh no, there were times when she would yell at bums who cussed at her and bothered customers. Or she would fight with a random person who would yell at her for dumb things like the cost of a can of soda. When stuff went down like that, Mom would cuss right back in her thick Korean accent: "You go out!" "You asshole!" "You son-of-bitch!" That being said, it was pretty rare that Mom got into fights. She tried her best to take the "customer-is-always-right" attitude. But when fights occurred and racial slurs got thrown around like a baseball in a game of catch, all I could think was that we all needed to watch what the fuck we said, but we didn't.

By early 1991, I was a full-fledged cashier and about to start the sixth grade. I was eleven years old and about five feet tall. My hair was long, and I was a little chubby. (I liked to eat). Mom trusted me to do shift changes, handle the inventory, and work on my own during graveyard shifts. On Saturday afternoons, I'd work the slow hours, and she'd take the busy noon traffic. On Sundays, we worked the cashier's booth together. Our shift began Saturday morning at 6 AM and ended on Sunday night at 10 PM. The cashier's booth is a small enclosure of roughly twenty-five feet long and ten feet wide. A large metal safe is tucked into the corner near the entrance. I used it as a makeshift table where I put my backpack. A metal wall with a small plastic window separates the booth from the back office. Mom kept that window covered with cardboard. The metal countertops are covered in candy bars, lighters, gum, mints, and other convenience items. The bulletproof windows have marks in them. One looks like a bullet hit the window. The other has a dent and a crack.

Photo of one bulletproof window facing Atlantic Avenue.
I've never confirmed if that is a bullet mark or not, but it
sure looks like it. (Photo from family archives).

So how did we end up with bulletproof windows? According to Mom, the story goes that when Dad first bought the Compton station in the mid-1970s, it didn't have bulletproof glass because the area was safer. In fact, Compton used to be a predominantly white city. But after racist housing practices were stopped by the Supreme Court and later the Watts Riots of 1965, the "white flight" of the residents of Compton changed the demographics of the city, and it became a predominantly black community in later years.[5] By the 1980s, manufacturing jobs left the area and contributed to the proliferation of drugs, gangs, and crime. The windows that protected the cashier's booth were now vulnerable to the growing violence in the area. Mom says that the windows were shattered during a late night argument with one of the workers and a man who was probably a gangster.

"You go out!" the worker said.

"Chink!" the gangster yelled back.

The guy thought he heard the worker call him a racist name. The worker claims he didn't say anything and only told the guy good night. That's when the argument ensued.

"I'm gonna come back here and shoot you," the man said to the worker.

"You leave!" the cashier said. "I'm going to call police!"

The gangster flipped the worker off and left. A few hours later, the guy came back. He was in a car with his buddies. He jumped out and pointed a gun at the worker. The thin glass window was the only thing separating them. The worker ducked as fast as he could. The gangster fired. The worker dropped to the floor. The window shattered. The gangster and his buddies drove off. Shards of glass were everywhere. Customers scattered like a flock of startled birds. The worker was curled up under the counter, his hands covering his head like he was practicing an earthquake drill. The glass had fallen all over him. Miraculously, he didn't get shot. After the incident, Dad decided to install bulletproof windows.

In the cashier's booth, I felt like I was watching the world go by, day by day, hour by hour, minute by minute, second by second. Everything I saw was different, odd, and sometimes downright traumatizing. One Saturday afternoon, I was standing in the booth, yet again, covering an hour for Mom while she talked to the mechanic and ordered inventory. I watched the flow of cars zooming through the intersection. I surveyed the property like Mom taught me to, checking for bums, threats, and anything that might be out of place. Something caught my eye in the distance. I looked across the street where I saw a long red line on the white paint of the column holding up the rival station's canopy. My eyes followed the stain slowly till I saw a black woman with short hair cropped to her chin slumped over on the ground. Her head was tilted to the right. Her eyes were closed. Customers walked by her, cars drove past; no one did or said anything to her from what I could see. I picked up the phone we had in the cashier's booth.

"911, what's your emergency?"

"There's a woman, I think she's hurt bad, there's blood, and she's not moving," I said.

"What's your location, ma'am?"

"I'm on Rosecrans Avenue in Compton," I said. "But the woman I'm talking about is across the street."

"How long has it been since you've seen the woman?"

"I just noticed her; it's been maybe a couple of minutes."

"We're sending someone right now."

I hung up the phone. Five minutes later a paramedic drove up to the station across the street. A few seconds after that a cop car parked at one of the pumps. The paramedic got out of his car and walked toward the woman. He bent down toward her and, with a light blue latex glove, tapped her. She didn't move. A cop, who had followed the paramedic, reached up to his shoulder walkie-talkie and said something.

"Hey," someone said from the other window. "Can I get twenty on number five?"

She surprised me, and I looked at her twice before I grabbed the money she had pushed into the tray. I turned on the pump. Another customer came to the window, and for a few minutes, while I dealt with them, I forgot what I had just seen. But when the line of customers stopped I immediately looked back to the scene. By this point, a coroner's van had showed up. A couple of guys were lifting the woman into a black body bag. The cop had a shovel and walked over to a grassy area near the sidewalk and dug up some dirt, walked back to where the woman had been, and threw the dirt on a pool of the woman's blood. People glanced at the situation; most ignored it and continued on their way. I would later hear from neighborhood folks that the woman had been stabbed in an attempted robbery. They said "attempted" because she still had her purse. But we will never know. When Mom came in to relieve me later so I could eat lunch, I told her what happened.

"And then the cops took her away," I finished.

"Did they come ask you questions?" she asked.

"No."

She grunted at me and told me not to think or worry about it anymore because it would just give me more stress.

"Get some food," she said.

I hadn't eaten anything since that morning at 5:30 AM when I practically inhaled a donut and a cup of coffee we picked up at a shop near our house. I called *Jugos Tropicales* and ordered a carne asada burrito with no onions and two tacos for Mom. Someone from the eatery delivered the food. I went to the back office and wolfed it down. Chewing my last bite, I went back to the cashier's booth and relieved Mom; she went to the garage to take care of some business. A customer walked up to the window and shoved a crumpled bill into the tray.

"What pump?" I asked as I unfolded the bill and gave her an annoyed look.

"What's your problem?" the woman asked as I stared at her.

"What number?" I said as I shoved the bill into the register and slammed it shut.

"Haven't you heard of customer service?"

"Number?" I said as I rolled my eyes.

"Stupid chink, you need to fix your attitude. Number nine," she said as she flipped me off and walked away.

I looked toward the woman as she pumped her gas. My mind raced. I tied my long black hair into a ponytail and rubbed the back of my neck. I stared at the boxes of multicolored gum: red, white, green, and blue. I picked up several sticks and stacked them into the shape of a house. I knocked them down with my chubby fist.

I felt alone in my bulletproof cashier's world. None of my friends could relate. I had only one black friend – Natalie – and she lived in Compton, just down the street from Mom's gas station. Her dad was the pastor of one of the local churches. To me, she wasn't one of those hateful customers that yelled at me. She was a school chum I talked to every now and then. Sometimes we traded tapes of Paula Abdul music. Sometimes we nodded our heads in acknowledgment of each other in the hall. We signed each other's yearbooks and gave each other our respective numbers, but we hardly ever called each other.

The kids I mostly hung out with were white. The private Christian school I went to was small, with less than twenty to thirty kids in each grade. By September 1991, I started my first year in middle school; the sixth grade. At this point I was a completely different person than I had been before Dad died. School was a strange place to me now. Where were the gangsters? Where were the pimps? School books were not inventory books. Friends were not angry customers.

"Carol, Mr. Smith would like to see you," I was told one day in class by my teacher.

I got up and straightened my dress. God, how I hated wearing dresses. I tried not to let the other kids make me feel bad for being called in by the principal. Mr. Smith had known my dad before he kicked the bucket and knew of Mom's difficult life. But what the heck did he want to see me for? *Hmm.* I thought about it for a few minutes. Did he hear about the fight I had with that girl Jane a few weeks ago? She slapped me, and during a tussle, I accidently pushed her down the stairs. No, really, it was an accident, though I think maybe she might have deserved it. Or, maybe he heard about how I cussed out some kid and told him he was a "jackass." Who knows? Who cared? It was a Friday and I wasn't looking forward to the weekend; I had to go to work with Mom.

I walked through the white-washed halls, making my way to the principal's office. It was quiet. Classes were in session. I took a moment to appreciate the solitude. No cars. No gas. No cigarettes to sell. It was nice. Mr. Smith greeted me when I got there. He had been waiting for me at the door. We walked into his small, square-shaped office. He had pictures of his family on his desk. The room had an old musty feel about it, and everything seemed brown. His desk was made of wood, and the walls were a brownish color. Even the freaking clock was brown. The picture frames were an off-brown, like sepia. I thought of the crayon and wondered why Mr. Smith liked brown so much. Or was it that all principal's offices were like this?

"Have a seat," he said.

I sat down in a chair next to his desk. And yes, the chair was light brown, dumb thing was also made of wood.

"I understand you've been under a lot of pressure lately," he started. "I want you to know that if you ever need to talk…"

Oh great, he was about to give me the "I will be there for you" bullshit. Same stuff I'd heard at Dad's funeral from friends of his who swore up and down the street that they'd be there for Mom and for me and my two older brothers. I never saw those guys again. Blah, blah, blah. Words, words, words. Useless words were coming out of his mouth. I nodded here and there just to give him some cue that I was paying attention. My mind wandered, and I thought about the station. How different his office was from my tiny cashier's booth. How silent it was. How calm it was despite all his blathering about caring.

"So on Monday I'd like to meet with your mother," he concluded.

"I don't think she'll be able to make it," I said. "She works a lot."

"Here's a note for her, please make sure you give it to her."

He handed me a sealed envelope with "Mrs. Park" written on it.

"Okay," I said as I put it in my pocket. "Can I go now?"

"I'm going to call your mom today and let her know that I sent you home with a letter," he said as he got up.

"Fine," I said.

He walked me to the door.

After school Mom picked me and my brothers up. We were only a year apart and attended the same school. I was in the sixth grade, Albert in seventh, and Tony in eighth. My brothers heard about the principal's inquisition and immediately asked me a thousand questions. I handed Tony the note.

"What did you do?" Mom asked after Tony explained what the letter said. Apparently, I was acting up in school, and Mr. Smith needed to speak with her.

"Nothing," I said. "I don't know why he wants to talk to you."

We drove home in silence as Mom mulled over how she would make time to meet with Mr. Smith. I thought about how the teachers at the school knew about Dad's death and wished they would stop trying to comfort me. The principal's wife even cornered me once during recess to check on how I was "feeling" and told me that "we're all here for you." Everyone knew my business, and I despised people's prying eyes and curiosity. When we got home, I ran upstairs to my room and plopped down on my twin mattress with the ugly orange and green blanket. The bright colors were so indicative of Korean culture. Darn thing stuck out like a sore thumb in my room. Thank God I never had any friends over. I emerged from my girl cave when Mom called us down for dinner. She had made rice, kimchi, and bulgogi. I savored the simple Korean meal. My brothers ate heartily.

The weekend shift was uneventful. Sure, I got into it with a few of the customers. Someone called me a gook. I called someone a beaner. Somebody else called me a nip, and I called that somebody a monkey.

On and on it went until we closed the shift Sunday night at 10 PM. I was grateful to be home. I showered and scrubbed away the smell of the booth – a weird mix of chocolate and gas. I went to my room, got into bed, and happily pulled my orange blanket over my head. I curled my toes into the sheets. Every Sunday night, after a long weekend at the gas station, I truly appreciated the simplicity of my lumpy mattress; it was way better than the gray tiled floor of the back office where I took my naps in a large green sleeping bag. Tucked under a large wooden desk in the office, that itchy green thing was warm, but it smelled like gas station, and I'm not sure if it had ever been washed. My mind wandered, and I started to fall asleep. I dreamed of the cashier's booth, the pumps, the cars, the inventory, and I could almost smell the dinginess of the station. Then I remembered. Mom and the principal were going to meet. Great, and here I thought I would have some peace.

In the morning, Mom accompanied my brothers and me to school. We got there early. Tony and Albert didn't come with us to the principal's office. It was a strange feeling walking in there with Mom. For a moment, I thought I was in *The Twilight Zone*. But alas, I was sitting in that lovely brown office again, wondering if it was just my imagination or if it had gotten browner over the weekend.

"Thank you for coming in, Mrs. Park. I know you're very busy," Mr. Smith said.

Mom was standing in front of him, her arms crossed. She looked impatient.

"What she do?" Mom asked in her thick Korean accent.

Most of the time I hated Mom's directness, but in that moment, I appreciated it.

"Well, it's complicated," Mr. Smith said. "Carol has been acting out at school. Albert has as well."

Mom let out an annoyed sigh.

"What they do?" she asked.

"I realize that your family has gone through a lot lately," Mr. Smith said. "After your husband died..."

Mom cut him off.

"What's problem?" she asked.

"It's not that there is a particular problem. It's more an observation and a recommendation I'd like to give you," he said. "I think it would be best if you took Albert and Carol to a therapist."

Mom's a respectful woman. Korean culture dictates that she shows deference and respect to teachers, elders, and those in positions of authority. But Korean culture also dictates that you don't share your family life with outsiders or "air your dirty laundry," so to speak. Mom didn't like it that the principal was interfering with her family affairs; after all, what did he know about Korean traditions, culture, and values?

"You waste time, you tell me this?" Mom said as she shook her head. "I go now."

"I didn't mean to waste your time," Mr. Smith said as Mom turned to leave. "Mrs. Park, it's just that your children are in need of some counseling."

"Okay, okay," Mom said. "I understanding. Thank you."

Mom left, and I gave Mr. Smith a shrug and followed her out the door.

"Behave yourself," Mom said to me in Korean as she got into her gray Mercedes-Benz. Dad had bought it for her right before he died. "Don't get into trouble. Don't waste my time."

"I'll be good," I said as she started the engine. "Bye."

Counseling. Wow. Seriously. Counseling? What the hell did the principal know about anything? Didn't he know it was normal for Korean kids like me to work with their parents? Didn't he know that Mom was one of the more than 28,000 Koreans who came to the United States in 1974, seeking the American Dream? That she lived through the kind of poverty that made eating grass sound tasty? Didn't he "understanding" that the difficult life we were having was a cakewalk compared to what Koreans lived through during and right after the Korean War? Who had the time and money to waste going to a therapist?

In retrospect, though, I wish Mom had taken his advice.

Chapter 3

A Cashier's Life

Trees lined the streets of my neighborhood. The two-story houses that were built in the 1970s have large front and back yards. Our driveway was huge – it could fit four cars – and the lawn was wide. There was a pool in the backyard I hardly used because I was always at the station. Plus, I can't swim too well, even to this day.

People watered their lawns in the evening, and neighbors chatted. Just one block away, outside of the neighborhood, is a large strawberry field. When Dad was alive, I'd doze to the smell of ripening berries during warm, lazy spring days. Upper-end chain stores and companies like Fedco called the city I used to live in their home. School districts fought to stay competitive, and private schools boasted about their programs and high college-placement rates. Back in the 1980s and 1990s, the population in the area was mostly white and Asian; it still is.

Compton, in the 1980s and early1990s, was predominantly black. The school near the station was run down, with broken windows, a small playground, and brown grass. Fences surrounded homes. Bars covered windows. Graffiti splashed street walls and billboards. Mom was constantly cleaning the station's white walls; they made perfect canvases for taggers.

In the area, there was a silent racism that we all lived by: Mexicans and Asians got along better than Asians and blacks; whites were cool with the Asians and Mexicans to a lesser extent but not so much with African Americans. Mexicans and blacks banded together when it was necessary against the whites and the Asians, and so it went on for years, a quiet alliance between races that no one dared to confirm or deny. We just lived that way. I lived that way.

The neighborhood next to the station is small. Mom knew most of the people around there, including an older gentleman who lives in a home behind the gas station. He's known Mom since the mid-1980s. Mom can't pronounce his real name, so she started calling him Eggo for short. It was like that for her distributor, Salam. She couldn't quite say his name right either. To his great dismay, she called him Saddam.

Eggo is a neighborhood godfather. Everyone knows him. He's the guy you ask if you need to find a market, the right check cashing place, or the best hole-in-the-wall restaurant. He's not the kind of "Don" Mario Puzo paints in his *The Godfather* stories; Eggo's the kind of man that helps without asking for "a service" in return. He's short in stature but has a big smile. He speaks little English. I learned my very first few Spanish words from him: *Hola. Buenos días. ¿Cómo estás?* His hair is that salt-and-pepper gray that makes you think of George Clooney.

Every Saturday morning, Eggo would walk by and say *hola* to me. Mom paid him a small stipend for his help around the station. Sometimes I'd give him some gum and soda. He emptied the trash bins, swept up the garbage, and cleaned the pumps. When he was done with his tasks, he'd sit on one of those wide, backyard-plastic-white chairs we kept around the garage bay for customers. He lounged around the station for most of the day and said hi to the customers that came and left. Some he knew. Some he didn't. At the same time, he kept an eye out for me and Mom.

Eggo's presence at the station made me feel a little safer. Saturdays weren't as hard to work because the garage bay was open, and the mechanic and Eggo were around. It was Saturday nights and Sundays I hated the most. That's when the drunks, gangsters, drug addicts, and pimps would come out to play. That's when the fights and threats were the worse.

"Shut up, kid, don't make me come back here and shoot you."

"Watch your back, gook, you gonna get hurt."

"You little chink, you best get out the hood."

Some nights were just hard. Especially in the winter, when the cold felt like a hard slap across the face. Yet there were days when I was shocked not by the racism and discrimination, but by Mom and her acquaintances. Once, in the mid-1990s. Mom surprised me when she went out of the booth on an early Sunday morning to greet a customer. Not but two minutes before, a nice car with gold rims, green felt on the hood, and dollar bills painted on the side pulled up to pump number five. I glanced at the driver.

Must be a gangster, I thought.

When Mom saw the car, she grabbed one of the new hats we were selling. She had a smile on her face. Confused, I gave her a questioning look. Before I knew what was happening, Mom made for the door. I was stunned. We hardly ever went outside when the mechanic's bay wasn't open. Mom and I heard one too many stories about her Korean friends being robbed during a shift change or in the early morning or late evening when no one was around. I stared out the cashier's window and watched as Mom made her way to the car. I wanted to follow her and tell her to stop – it was dangerous – but before I could work up the courage, she was already greeting the customer.

"Hullo!" Mom said. "Wow, you have new car!"

"Well, hello there, Mrs. Park," the man said as he got out of the nice car and leaned on his beautifully polished cane. "It's so very nice to see you again. How are you?"

"Good," she said. "You look good today!"

"Why, thank you," he said as he took a few steps toward the hood of the car where Mom was standing. "You been workin' all night?"

"Yes, but it not bad," she said.

"Always working hard," he said as he patted Mom on the shoulder. He was much taller than she was, and the long purple fur coat he was wearing made him look even bigger.

"No, you working hard, too, always here in morning," she said.

He laughed. Mom lifted up the orange and blue hat and showed it to him.

"Well now, what have we got here?" he asked.

"This for you," she said. "It's hat for you. You always have nice hat, so I give you one."

"For me?" he said politely. "Why, thank you!"

As he spoke, he set his cane against the hood and took off his purple hat, which had a light-colored feather tucked in a leopard band that circled the rim. He set his hat down on the hood of the car, taking care not to get it dirty. Mom handed him the new one. He took it from her with a certain amount of grace that made it seem like he was receiving an award. He puffed the fold of it out and, with one hand, put it on. As he adjusted the fit, he took his forefinger and thumb and pinched the edge of the hat, ran his fingers across the length, and smiled.

"That's a perfect fit," he said.

"Oh, you like it," Mom said. "It look good on you."

"I'm going to keep this, Mrs. Park, and wear it whenever I get a chance," he said.

Flabbergasted at what I had just seen and realized – Mom was friends with a pimp – I stared at them wondering how and when Mom got to know that character. I watched as the pimp took off the gift Mom gave him, picked up his cane, and put his purple hat back on. Mom pointed to his car as they continued their conversation.

"This is pretty car," she said. "You even paint dollar bill on side, you very successful."

"Nah, I just try to earn my keep," he said as he started to come my way. "Hey, is that your daughter?"

Mom nodded her head yes as she made her way with him toward the cashier's booth. Amazed, a jumble of thoughts went through my head as I watched them walk toward me. *Who is this guy? How did they meet?! Hope there won't be trouble.*

"Well now, she looks like you," he said as he showed me his golden smile. "How are you, young lady?"

"Fine, sir," I said. "It's nice to meet you."

"Me and your mom, we go way back. I've been coming here for years. She's always hookin' it up."

As he spoke, he pulled out his bank roll; a bunch of twenty and hundred dollar bills. He fished out a twenty and dropped it in the tray.

"Number five, sweetie," he said.

"Sure. Thank you. Do you need anything else?" I asked.

"Nah, sugar, I'm good."

Mom patted his arm and said thank you. I had never seen her touch a customer's arm or hand before. She had taught me that it was rude in Korean culture to do that; to touch the hands of customers while giving change or stare them in the eyes. But here she was not following the rules and regulations she laid out for me when I first started working at the station. When she came back inside the booth I stammered out several questions.

"Who is that? How do you know him? Why have I never seen him before? He looks shady."

Mom shook her head at me as if to scold my lack of knowledge. Then she told me in Korean, "He is a long-time customer. He always comes to get his car fixed here. You never seen him because you are in school or you aren't working the day he comes. He spends a lot of money fixing his cars, buying gas, cigarettes, and many other things. He is also a nice man, very nice to me and the mechanic. He doesn't cause trouble."

"Mom, you have to be careful, you can't just go outside like that. You

30

always tell me not to go outside when it's only us working. Why did you do that? I don't care if it's the President, please don't do that again."

"You don't understand nothing," she said. "He's a good customer, what he does for work isn't my business. He's a nice man, and he comes here all the time. I treat him well because he treats me well. I gave him a hat because this is good business practice, this is customer service."

I decided to see what the pimp was doing instead of engaging in more business lessons with Mom. The pimp was screwing in the gas cap. He glanced toward the booth and caught my eye. I waved. He tipped his hat. That pimp would come to the station every now and then for years. Eventually, he stopped coming by. Mom thinks he got arrested or killed. Whenever I tell this story, I always add in the disclaimer: "No, he's not my father."

When I wasn't fighting with customers or realizing Mom knew pimps and gangsters, and when things weren't racially charged, I'd sit and observe the world and people around me. I'd watch as cars marched by like a line of ants. Cars with those cool hydraulics. Cars with tints so dark, you couldn't see anything inside. I'd watch people walking by. Some looked frazzled. Others had a purpose. Mothers looked strong, making their way to the local market.

Sometimes I was surprised by the random things people said, asked for, or tried to sell me while I was working. Random thugs and hustlers would try to peddle me things like: clothes, watches, rings, speakers, necklaces, and other cool stuff I'm sure was stolen. Sometimes, I'd be shocked by what people strolled by with, or what they did, or even at the random violence I saw.

Once, a car with three guys pulled up to one of the pumps. One of them got out with a beer in his hand and a joint in the other; I prayed he would put it out before pumping the gas. He did.

One day a motorcycle was exiting the 7-Eleven at the corner of Rosecrans Avenue. As the motorcyclist pulled out of the driveway, a car making a right didn't notice and slammed into him. The guy flew off his bike and landed three feet away. His shiny black and white helmet smacked the ground. I know I couldn't have possibly heard it, but I swear I almost did because he hit the ground so hard. Several people rushed to his aid and stopped oncoming traffic. I picked up the phone and called 911. People gathered around the man and kept him stable. A few minutes later, the paramedics showed up and took him away.

One morning, around 6 AM, two prostitutes walked up to the booth. As they bought cigarettes and lighters, a big purple suburban pulled up. The car had the latest tire rim fad; spinner hubcaps. The two women started screaming and yelling, "Oh my God! Look at that ride! Look at them spinners!" Then they approached the car. One of them got in.

One night, while Mom was sleeping in the back, a pimp – not the one we knew – pulled up to pump number ten in a copper-colored car. He jumped out and grabbed a woman that was walking by; she was pretty, wearing high heels and a short, light blue dress. Her brown hair was streaked with blond. The pimp slapped her once across the face, said something, and shoved her into the car. All I could think was, *Damn these people and their violence.*

On yet another late night, a drunk lady pulled into the station around 2 AM. She was smiling and looked happy. She slurred her words as she asked for a few dollars on pump number one. I turned the gas on for her and hoped she would make it home safely and not kill anyone on the way. As I sat back down on my seat, I watched the woman put the nozzle in her car. After a few seconds, she got into her vehicle and closed the door. I heard her engine turn on. Before I could get to the gas station's speaker system and yell at her to stop, she drove off. The nozzle tore away from the hose as the lady sped away. Gas spewed everywhere.

"Mom!" I yelled. "Mom, some lady just drove off with the pump in her car! There's gas all over!"

Mom came rushing into the booth. She hit the big red button she told me never to touch except in emergencies. In the early 1990s, we didn't have safety break latches that stopped gas from spilling everywhere whenever someone drove off with the pump still in the car; by 1997, we had those installed. It was amazing how many times someone would just drive off with the pump still connected. It happened at least once a month.

At night, when crazy things weren't happening, Mom and I talked. I'd tell her about what I saw. She'd tell me to not worry about it. I'd tell her that customers were mean, and I hated being there at the station. She'd say don't complain. I'd say black people keep cussing at me, and it's not right.

She'd say don't cause trouble and switch the subject. Sometimes she gave me lessons on my Korean heritage.

"When you're older, you must get married, respect your mother-in-law, and take care of your children. If you act like this now, getting mad so easily at customers, cussing, and acting so stupid, you will shame me. Don't shame me."

I'd always disregard her efforts to teach me about my Korean heritage. I didn't care at the time. She tried to tell me about Korean history and why she came to the United States. How having the two-story home in the middle-class neighborhood we lived in was a dream she could have never realized in Korea because when she was growing up in the 1950s and 1960s, her family was so poor she had to walk two miles to the mountains just to find wild melons to eat. She tried to tell me about how lucky me and my brothers were to be able to have food so readily available from fast food joints and from grocery stores. I just didn't listen.

Most of my Saturday nights and Sundays were riddled with small arguments and friendly banter with some of the locals I knew, including one woman who always came to buy menthol cigarettes. She was a teacher and loved to wear her hair in long braids with blonde highlights. She was nicer to me than most of my teachers at school. I liked her better than I liked the principal.

People like that teacher lived in or around the city of Compton. The station borders the cities of Lynwood and Paramount and attracted customers from around there as well. When I started working at the station, I didn't know how bad Compton was, nor did I understand the violent history the city had. In 1988, the city was made even more notorious when the rap group N.W.A. released their song "Straight Outta Compton."

Overall, the layout of the station was nice. Little orange and white placards with the numbers 1-12 sit far above each pump, like markers on a map. A big orange ball serves as a makeshift lighthouse for customers at night. The dark blue of the numbers sharply contrast with the orange and catches the attention of drivers as they pass by. Inside the single building of the gas station, the cashier's booth connected to the office via a small hallway on one side. A bathroom adjoined the other side. We didn't let customers in to use it because it was too dangerous, especially at night. On Atlantic Avenue, there's a donut shop, a non-brand name 99 cents store, a grocery market, and a Chinese restaurant. On Rosecrans Avenue there is a convenience store and the rival gas station.

Working at the gas station opened my eyes to a world of knowledge I would have never learned at school. During, the first two years I worked at the station – 1990 and 1991 – I learned how prevalent drugs were in the area. In the 1980s, the drug turf wars between the Bloods and the Crips fueled the violence and mayhem. The influx of the latest drug – crack cocaine – became the tinder to fuel the flames of violence and crime that spread throughout South Central Los Angeles. Koreans were caught in the crossfire as the "middleman minority" of society.

People in the area smoked crack like crazy.

"Give me a flower," a customer said to me one night. I didn't know what he was referring to.

"Sorry, we don't have those," I said.

Over the next several weekend shifts, people kept asking for flowers or roses. Mom finally started to sell them after I told her how many customers I turned away. The cute little glass pipes had a paper or plastic flower inside with foil or cork covering the ends. I thought they were nice little gifts. I even took a purple one with me and kept it in my backpack to show the other kids at school.

I sold a whole box of roses in one shift. Curious about the popularity of the small glass flower, I started asking customers what they were for. Most said nothing. Some said the roses were great presents for girlfriends. Some laughed at my question and walked away. One day, a random customer finally answered me.

"Flowers? That's for crack, girl!" a middle-aged man said.

"What's that?" I asked.

"Crack is the poor man's drug," he said with a smile. "Crack is what we do around here cause the white powder costs too much."

The tube is used as a crack pipe, he explained. The paper flower inside the glass is blown out and a small piece of copper scouring pad – commonly referred to as a "screen" – is inserted. People use lighters to smoke the drug. The screen acts as a filter. Users inhale the vapors and get high for up to fifteen minutes.

"So why do you always buy the roses?" I asked the middle-aged man.

"Cause it don't last," he said.

The short pipes, after heavy use, end up cracking or breaking.

"How long do they last?" I asked.

"That depends how much you smokin'," he said. "If you got the ends, you probably be smokin' lots so you'd be going through them pipes like they was candy."

I handed him his flower and thanked him.

"You have a good one, sister," he said as he walked away.

Glass flowers got popular in the early 1990s. The man I talked to about the pipes was just one of a few hundred I'd seen over the years addicted to drugs, especially crack. I had regulars who would come by and purchase flowers at least once a week. Some came every few days. Those pipes sold like hotcakes. In a sixteen-hour shift, I'd sell two boxes of flowers, or roses as they were sometimes called; each box contained thirty-six, 4-inch tubes. There was a lot of drug use going on in our neighborhood and in other inner cities. We weren't the only shop in the area selling roses. The market, the 99 cents store, and the other station across the street all had them in stock. I sold roses to people from every walk of life. Some days I'd sell them to moms, some days it was to men in suits, and some days it was to dads.

A box of those crack pipes cost about $10 wholesale, maybe more or less, but I can't remember. We sold each rose for a dollar and made $36 a box. We sold around two boxes a day and took in about $52 in profit. I couldn't help but marvel at the economy that drugs supported. Drug use boosted sales for businesses that sold the right items and supported manufacturers and the distributors who deliver the products to stores. Those manufacturers and distributors hire workers who in turn make a wage that they use to pay rent, buy food, and clothes. Drug money essentially floats around in every aspect of people's lives and supports, or really, subsidizes local, national, and international economies. Think of drug trafficking around the world: from places like Columbia to the United States, to Asia, and to Europe. At least that's what I learned while sitting in my bulletproof cashier's booth, watching drug dealers, selling roses and screen, and doing the math.

I'd watch once healthy, vibrant regulars turn into shadows of themselves as their addictions took control of their lives. They got thin, their lips blistered, and they looked dirty. They lost their jobs. They lost

35

their families. Eventually I'd stop seeing them all together. Watching the downward spiral of these once strong, motivated people made me stay away from drugs; I didn't want to end up like that. Besides, at school they had just run the Nancy Regan "Just Say No" campaign. I couldn't imagine my teachers marching around at the station with "Just Say No" signs, shirts, and posters. Drug use was so prominent in the area that at times I'd see people take a hit right there at the gas station.

"Tony, what do you think that guy is doing?" I asked during one of our marathon weekend shifts. "He's been in his car for ten minutes."

My oldest brother, who was trying to study while I took my turn at the register, walked over and looked out the window. I was glad he decided to come and help that weekend. I was glad someone else was there to suffer with me! The man we saw was at pump one. We could clearly see him just sitting in his car. As we watched, the man lifted a pipe up to his mouth. He thumbed a lighter with his other hand; the flame lit up the inside of his car. Tony shook his head.

"What's going on?" I asked.

"He's probably smoking crack."

The man laid his head back as the high kicked in.

It always shocked me to see people doing drugs at the station. It's one thing to see people taking a drink from a forty, but it's another to see guys smoking crack or weed, or doing some other form of narcotics right before hitting the road. I used to think that I should call the police and report these druggies. I tried to a couple of times but nothing ever happened. Eventually, I decided that I would save my 911 calls for bigger problems. As the night wore on, Tony and I talked about school. Business was slow. Several minutes passed until finally someone came to the window.

"Hey man," Tony said. "What can I get you?"

The black guy looked at my brother for a moment. I was standing near the doorway in the hall, and out of sight. I was taking my break as my brother took his turn at the register. Mom was still sleeping in the back office.

"How ya doin'?" the man asked my brother.

"It's late," Tony said.

"You know, if you need a little somethin', I can help you out," the guy said as he reached into his jacket pocket.

He opened up his palm and showed the contents to Tony.

"What's that?" Tony asked.

"It's crack, boy," the man said. "You want some? I'll hook you up."

"No, thanks, man," Tony said as he waved a hand at the guy. "That's not my thing."

"What? You watchin' too many of them afterschool specials or somethin'?" the guy joked.

"Nah, I'm studying," Tony said as he lifted up his science textbook.

"It's cool, kid," the guy pressed. "This stuff will make you feel good."

"My mom would kill me," Tony said.

The guy shrugged his shoulders.

"Fine," he said as he turned and started to walk away. "Someday, maybe."

Tony turned and looked at me.

"Did you see that?" Tony asked. "Did you see those crystals in his hand?"

"Remember, 'Just Say No to Drugs,' brother!" I joked.

Crack wasn't the only prevalent drug in the area. In later years, methamphetamines became popular, too. That being said, marijuana was the one drug that never lost its popularity. The use of cannabis supported our sales of flavored cigars and tobacco wraps. In fact, I've never seen a customer buy a flavored cigar and smoke it for its intended purpose. Instead, I'd see people dump out the tobacco of the cigar and put their ground-up kush inside, right there at the station. They'd light up in their cars and then drive away. Flavored cigars sold like candy. Once, we sold so many during our weekend shift, we ran out of them. Mind you, one box contained fifty pieces, and Mom usually kept ten boxes around for the weekend. (That's five hundred cigars!) Sitting in that booth, I learned so much about things like drugs and violence. While these are not skills per se, they did open my eyes to the world and made me see beyond the walls of my nice home and my sheltered private school.

Another thing I learned was how to entertain myself in that shitty little booth. I'd do homework. I'd read. Sometimes I built fortresses made out of gum sticks. Sometimes I stacked soda cans so high that they reached the top of the windows. Sometimes I took the cigarette packs and arranged them into colorful displays. Mom would get mad at me and tell me to stop messing around with the inventory. Sometimes I'd fold origami. Sometimes I imagined emergency scenarios and how I would get out of them. Sometimes I'd talk to customers and ask them questions like: "What's that cigar for?" "What kind of car is that?" "What are you eating?" Mostly though, I'd sit there on that little blue cushioned seat and stare off into space until someone would startle me out of my boredom.

"Hey, one of those boxes," said a Mexican man one cool summer night in 1991. Confused, I looked at him. I had no idea what he was talking about.

"That red box behind you."

I turned around to look at the wall. Sure enough there were red and blue boxes hanging from a little bar sticking out of one of the slats. Mom forgot to tell me that she added them to the inventory. I took one of the red boxes down and looked for the price. Mom had scribbled $2.49 on the top right corner with a black marker. I dropped the box in the metal tray as he gave me the money. When he left, I picked up a box.

"Non-lubricated, premium latex condoms," I read.

I flipped the box over.

These "condoms are made from premium quality latex to help reduce the risk of unwanted pregnancy and sexually transmitted diseases. Each condom is electronically tested to help ensure reliability. More Americans trust [this] brand more than any other condom."

Sexually transmitted diseases? Pregnancy? What?!

I put the box back and looked around to make sure there were no more customers. I walked over to the back office where Mom was eating a very late dinner; it was 11 o'clock.

"Mom, what are condoms for?"

She put her chopsticks down and looked at me.

"They are for men to use," she said. "Why?"

"Because you didn't tell me we were selling them. I just sold one. I don't know what they are."

"Well, don't think about it. Okay? Go back to the booth."

"Uh huh," I said as I resolved to just ask a customer instead.

I went back to the booth and sat down on my chair. I watched random cars drive down Atlantic Avenue and waited. A few customers trickled in here and there and bought gas, gum, and candy. After a couple of hours, a black man walked up to the window and asked for a box of condoms.

I grabbed one.

"Two forty-nine," I said.

As he dropped his three dollars into the tray, I looked at him, ready to ask my question. He wasn't looking at me and probably didn't want to talk, but I asked anyway.

"Sir?" I asked. "What are condoms for?"

He kept his head down and waited for me to give him his change.

"Sir?" I insisted.

He fidgeted with his jacket. I stood there, holding the condoms in one hand and the change in the other.

"Uh, well, yeah, those are for couples," he said. He shifted his feet and looked down as he spoke.

"What do you mean?" I asked.

"You know, for a man and a woman, when they want to sleep together."

What? Condoms are small blankets? I thought.

"I don't understand," I said.

"Well, you know, when people wanna have sex."

Sex was something I knew next to nothing about. We never talked about sex at the private Christian school I went to, and Mom certainly never mentioned it to me. I thought it was stuff like kissing and holding hands. I was thoroughly confused. Why would people need to buy something just to hold hands and kiss?

"What's that?" I asked the man.

"Girl, I don't wanna be the one to tell you that. Can I get my change?"

Disappointed, I gave him his fifty-one cents and the box of condoms. He quickly walked away. Still befuddled, I went to the back office again. Mom was reading the Korean paper.

"Mom?"

"Uh-huh?"

"What's sex?"

I saw her body tense up. She folded the paper and set it on the table as she turned to look at me.

"What?"

"One of the customers just told me that condoms are for sex. I don't understand."

"You don't need to understand," she said. "Just sell it and don't ask questions."

"But I want to know," I protested.

"Stop bothering me, and go back and watch the booth."

"Fine," I said.

She was too embarrassed to tell me what condoms were really for. I was still too young to know that kind of stuff at the time; I was only eleven. I finally learned what sex was after I asked some older kids at school. But, I didn't fully understand the whole picture until I was a freshman attending a public high school and sex education was mandatory.

Mom never really explained stuff like that to me. She was a proper Korean woman and instead of telling me about things like sex or puberty, she made sure that I knew how to cook, clean, and be a dutiful Korean daughter. She grew up with the Confucian ideologies that are prominent in Korean culture to this day. Family is the center of our universe. The oldest son is like the prince and is expected to take care of the parents in their old age. Daughters like me are taught to be good cooks because if you can't cook, how can you be useful? We're also taught that taking care of the children and husband is the main duty of the wife. The wife and mother sacrifices herself for the well-being of the family, no matter what. A daughter trains her whole life to do this and bring honor to her family. If a girl marries an oldest son, she is also responsible for taking care of her husband's parents. The mother-in-law rules the roost. Mom always made sure I understood these things. When Mom told me this kind of stuff, I'd say ok.

My ethnic heritage both confused me and fascinated me. I grew up speaking Korean with Mom and English with Dad. He believed my brothers and I should be raised as Americans. That's why I don't have a Korean name. Dad wanted us to be fully immersed in the American culture. Mom, however, believed we were both Korean and American at the same time and didn't want us to lose our traditions. Before Dad died, I embraced my Americanness. I didn't fully understand my Korean blood until I started working at the station, and it was thrown in my face day in and day out. I had never known slanted eyes could be such an issue.

Chapter 4

The Yellow Brick Road

So how did my family end up owning a business in Compton? How did Koreans end up there and in other inner cities? When my parents were children, they were growing up in the aftermath of the Korean War (1950-1953). An armistice agreement, which established a ceasefire between North and South Korea, left both sides in a quagmire of poverty. Mom and Dad knew hunger, and they knew the bitterness of a harsh winter's night.

American soldiers were left to guard the 38th parallel, also known as the Demilitarized Zone (DMZ). The zone separates North and South Korea. Korean women, like Mom's cousin, met and married American servicemen who were stationed in the South to help guard the DMZ. Then, a few years later, in 1965, the passage of the Immigration and Nationality Act opened the door for Koreans to immigrate to America. In 1964, 2,362 Koreans migrated to the US. By 1974 that number jumped to a total of 28,028.[6] Mom's cousin sponsored her under the new terms of the immigration act. So in 1974, Mom bid farewell to her six brothers and sisters, looked her father in the eye one last time, and made her way to Los Angeles.

"I know I will never see you again," Grandfather told her. "I should have been better to you. I love you."

When Mom got to Los Angeles, she was faced with a world she didn't know and had never heard about from Koreans back home. In the 1970s, discrimination was still prominent, and Koreans, like most of the other minorities, were denied corporate jobs. Mom ended up working as a seamstress at a clothing shop. By the 1970s, the Jewish community and Japanese community had begun to sell their inner-city businesses and move to newer neighborhoods, especially after the 1965 Watts Riots. That's when Koreans turned to buying those stores. Some Koreans invested money in opening wig shops and liquor stores in places like South Central Los Angeles, Chicago, and New York.

When Mom met Dad – they lived in the same apartment complex in California – she had found her paradise. Together they lived in the land of milk and honey. They could raise their children to be fat and happy. (And believe you me, I was fat). They worked hard and earned enough money that they didn't have to worry about things like food and clothes. To Mom, America is the Promised Land; it's the place where Spam and ketchup overflow, where sunshine stokes the fires of happiness. America is the place she dreamed about as a child, starving on a farm in the small countryside of Kwangju, South Korea.

As my parents worked, the racial tension between Koreans and blacks brewed. For twenty-some-odd years, the conflict was exacerbated by incident after incident. Media coverage fanned the flames of trouble as stories pitted one minority against the other.[7] When I started working in the cashier's booth, the tension was at its tipping point.

For Mom, however, the problems were just a part of what she had to deal with, and she did her best to avoid it. To her, having a business was a blessing despite all the fear, racism, and violence. She couldn't provide for me and my brothers, put food on the table, or send us to school if she didn't have that gas station in Compton. So gangs, drug wars, and shootings didn't scare her. Racism and discrimination didn't bother her, even though it sure as hell bothered me. I was sick of the station. I resented that my life was a cycle of shift change after shift change, racist slur after racist slur.

"I'm not going!" I said to her one day. "You do it! Take Tony or Albert. I'm not going!"

Mom let out a sigh as she picked up the rice cooker and put it in a box.

"You get ready," she said. "I need you to help me this weekend."

"No," I said as I thumped my fist on the kitchen table.

"We don't have a lot of time. Stop arguing with me," she said.

"What the hell?!" I said. "I just said no! I'm not going there. I'm staying home!"

"Don't cuss," she said.

"This shit isn't fair!"

"Stop cussing," she said as she started to get mad.

"This shit's illegal! I'm just a kid!" I said as I stood up. "You can't make me go!"

She smacked the back of my head. I probably shouldn't have cussed. But my hormones were running amuck and I was probably on a period-induced rampage. Whatever the case, I still feel like I was justified. She shouldn't have smacked me.

"What the hell?!" I yelled as I rubbed my head.

She smacked me again.

"Ow! Ow! Okay, okay!" I said. "Stop it!"

"No, you stop it," she said. "Don't say bad words, and hurry up and get ready."

Subdued by Mom's momentary lapse in parental judgment, I went to my room and got ready for our shift. The relationship Mom and I have is always filled with straightforward, blunt comments, unsaid feelings, and moments like that. Instead of saying "I love you" or "thank you," Mom would just do stuff because she assumed I already knew that she cared. That's just the Korean way, or at least that's what she made me think. Sometimes she'd buy me things like a new, oversized vest from one of the distributors with the disclaimer, "This will keep you warm while you work." And when we'd eat our dinner of cold Korean side dishes and rice at the station, she'd always give me the last bit of whatever it was we had.

"Don't worry, I'm done," she'd say. "You eat a lot. Do you want more rice?"

I'd nod, and she'd scoop some more of the steamy Calrose grains into my bowl. One of the things Mom and I always brought with us to the station was a small rice cooker. At night Mom would wash the rice in the bathroom sink and cook it in the back office. We'd have rice, kimchi, and whatever side dish we happened to snag on our way out. We couldn't run across the street to the Chinese food place for dinner, as it closed around 8 PM. (Besides, we'd already eaten from there for lunch). We had to fend for ourselves at night during the graveyard shift. We didn't dare venture out to the local taco shop at night either; it was too dangerous and they didn't always deliver past a certain hour.

Working at the booth was a constant in my life. No occasion, no holiday or vacation ever gave Mom cause to stop working in that booth during the weekends. She couldn't afford to hire someone or pay overtime. The station was open twenty-four hours a day, and we had no choice but to cover those weekend shifts; that's how Mom saved enough money to pay the mortgage, sock some away for my brothers' and my college fund, and still pay the bills. In fact, many Korean shop owners put their kids to work for the same reasons as Mom. So, I spent several of my birthdays and holidays staring at the big gold-rimmed clock in the cashier's booth. I fought with customers, gorged on candies, and thought about how when

I turned eighteen, I'd go away to college and never have to work at that stinking rat hole of a booth again.

Holidays and birthdays turned into cashier booth festivities. All I did was work and go to school. When Dad was alive, birthdays were fun. There was always cake, and I'd get to go on Toys' R Us shopping sprees. Those were different times.

"It's still my birthday," I said to Mom in the car as we drove home from the station one night. (I think it was my thirteenth or fourteenth birthday; I can't remember exactly).

"I know," Mom said. "Happy birthday."

It was a little past 10 PM. *Is there going to be a cake?* I thought. As we made our way home, Mom didn't take the usual exit. Instead, she pulled into a shopping complex that had a bakery.

"Wait here," she said as she got out. "Don't let anyone in."

After a few minutes, she came back with a cake box. I smiled, grateful for Mom's effort after our crazy long shift. We went home. Tony and Albert were waiting up for us. Mom told them to go to the big glass dining table in the living room and set out some plates. She took the yellow box and put it on the table. We all sat down.

"Tony, get some candles," Mom said.

He scrounged around the kitchen, opening drawers, looking in cabinets; he couldn't find a single one. Mom got up to help.

"Happy birthday, Carol," Albert said as we waited. "Aren't you tired?"

"Yeah," I said. "I want some cake."

Mom came back to the dining room with Tony. She had a long-tapered candle in her hand. It was one of the candles we used during Dad's annual memorial. (We honored the Korean ancestral rights tradition of making food, setting it out in front of Dad's picture, lighting candles and basically – like Día de los Muertos – we feed the dead). Mom took the flaxen-colored candle and stuck it in the center of the cake. She grabbed a lighter and lit it. They sang the birthday song. I blew out the flame. Mom cut it.

"Why does it look like that?" I asked.

The cake fell apart as mom tried to slice a piece.

"It smells," Albert said. "What kind of cake is this?"

Mom dabbed at the mushy lump with a finger. She tasted it and then put it back down.

"It's rotten," she said.

I sighed.

"Happy birthday, me," I said.

Mom cleared the table. I went up to my room. I lay down on my bed and pulled my orange blanket over my face. I leaned my head against the wall and curled up into a ball. I loved my flower print sheets and the coolness of the pillowcase against my cheek. I savored the quiet of my dark room. As I drifted, I thought of bullets, cuss words, candy bars, and rotten, mushy cake.

Holidays at the station were never fun either. Mom and I often worked on Thanksgiving, Christmas, New Year's Eve, and New Year's Day. The first time I worked the graveyard with Mom on New Year's Eve, I learned about the velocity of bullets and basically had my first physics lesson: what goes up, must come down.

"Happy New Year's Eve," I said to Mom in Korean as I sat down on the blue cushioned seat next to the register. It was about 11:30 PM on New Year's Eve in 1990. Mom had given the worker the night off. I was on winter break, so she took me to the station with her. Mom was standing in the cashier's booth with me, looking at the cigarettes, checking to see what needed to be stocked.

"Do you need anything?" she asked.

"Yeah, a box of chocolate and some gum."

Mom wandered to the back office. She came back with the items and some cartons of cigarettes.

"It's pretty slow right now," I said as I put the gum in its place.

"Well, it's New Year's Eve," Mom said.

Time flew as Mom and I stocked inventory. Soon it was midnight. As the first few seconds of the New Year ticked away, I heard loud popping sounds. Shot after shot. Bang after bang. I ducked under the counter and yelled at Mom to do the same.

"Get down!" I screeched.

"It's okay," she said. "Come out. No one's firing at us. It's just people shooting their guns in the air."

"Are you sure?" I asked.

"Yes," Mom said. "Stop being stupid. Come here and help me."

Relieved, I climbed back into my chair.

"Why would people do that?" I asked as I tried to calm my nerves.

"They're celebrating," Mom said as she ripped up cigarette cartons. We use the blank insides as scratch paper; it was our way of recycling.

"Isn't that dangerous?" I asked as I helped her tear up the cartons. "Won't the bullets come down?"

"Yes, but they're not firing at the gas station," Mom said.

"Wow," I said. "That's still crazy."

That night, whether it was just imagination or reality, I don't know, but I thought I could hear the thud of bullets hitting the station's canopy. After all, we were located right next to a neighborhood of gun-toting, happy people celebrating the New Year.

It wasn't until many years later that I truly understood how dangerous it is to shoot guns straight up in the air. In fact, 118 people were treated for injuries resulting from falling bullets at King/Drew Medical Center in Los Angeles County from 1985 to 1992, according to a *Los Angeles Times* article.[8] Thirty-eight of those people died. Those who survived ended up with major health problems. Some had paraplegia, quadriplegia, seizures, chronic pain, and more. Apparently, injuries from falling bullets happened the most around New Year's and the Fourth of July. For me, working holidays sucked.

"Mom," I said one year during our New Year's Eve shift. "We need to think about putting metal plates on the roof of the station. I don't want to die from a falling bullet."

She didn't listen to me. She argued that we never had a problem with falling bullets, just the ones that randomly flew by, and really, there wasn't much we could do about those anyway. What's the point of spending so much money on something that wasn't going to make a difference? Mom just didn't think bullets could hit the station's canopy. Years later, we'd find out otherwise.

"Mom, the roofer wants to talk to you," I said to her one Saturday afternoon. "He's waiting for you."

I had wandered to the back office where Mom was resting. I'd just taken over the shift from her. The roofer had come to fix a leak in the canopy after a particularly bad storm. Mom followed me back to the booth so she could talk with the roofer.

"Hi, Mrs. Park," the man said. "We just finished patching the leak."

"Thank you," Mom said in her Korean accent. "Everything okay now?"

"Yeah," the roofer said. "You should know, though, that we found a lot of bullet holes and even some bullets up there. You should think about putting up some extra plating."

Ha! I thought. *I knew it! Those bullets do hit the canopy! I'm not just hearing things!*

To my great dismay, Mom never put the metal plating up.

I worried a lot about our safety, and not just from falling bullets. I worried about getting shot, getting robbed, and getting hurt, especially as the racial tension got worse and worse between Koreans and blacks. Every time Mom and I got out of the car and walked those few feet to the cashier's booth, I sweated. What if someone tried to rob us? What if there was a drive-by? What if someone finally decided they didn't like that Korean woman and her daughter? What if, what if...

"What's going on?" I asked one late evening on a school night at home. I walked into Mom's room. "Who called?"

"Go back to bed," Mom said.

I rubbed my eyes and saw that Tony and Albert were also awake and sitting next to her. They had heard the phone ring, too.

"What happened?" I asked Albert.

"The police just called. The workers got stabbed," he said. "We need to go to the station."

Shocked, I shook my head.

"Are they okay?" I asked. "Are they alive?"

"Yes," Tony said. "They got taken to the hospital."

"Can I go to the station with you guys?" I asked.

"No," Mom said. "Go back to sleep."

"There's nothing you can do," Albert added as he adjusted his glasses.

"Are you going to the station right now?" I asked.

"Yeah, me and Mom are going," Albert said.

Tony and I sat on the stairs and waited for them to leave. I couldn't believe that the workers had been stabbed! *By who? Why?* When they left, I went to my room and tried to go back to sleep. Instead, my head was filled with random thoughts and scenarios. What if it had been me and Mom? What would I do if someone tried to stab me? How could I defend myself in that small cashier's booth where I could hardly move? It was so cramped in there that if I had been a larger, wider person, I couldn't have fit, much less fought off a would-be attacker. Mom and Albert didn't come back until it was past 6 AM. Mom made us breakfast, and I peppered her with questions. She looked worn.

"What happened?" I asked as she fried some eggs.

"The workers were doing a shift change," she said as she flipped the eggs over. "One of them went outside to do the meter reading, and when he was going back inside the booth, a black man came running up to them and pushed them inside. He had a knife."

Mom took a plate out from the cupboard.

"Get me the bread," she said.

I grabbed the loaf from the counter and handed it to her. She started to make toast in the pan, just the way I liked it; buttered and fried to a golden brown.

"So some dude pushed his way into the booth?" I asked as Mom cooked.

"Yes," she said. "The man told the workers to give him all the money and then he threatened them with the knife."

The two workers shoved the guy as he started to attack them. The money had already been dropped into the large metal safe at the corner of the booth. There was only one hundred dollars in the cashbox and some loose bills lying out next to the register. The robber didn't know that the money was already in the safe, so he tried to stab the workers to get to the register. Fearing for their lives, the two male workers fought the robber. As they struggled in the booth, one of the workers grabbed a metal bat that was stashed next to the safe.

The robber cut and stabbed the workers as he reached for the money on the counter. During the tussle, one of the workers hit the guy in the head repeatedly with the bat. Dazed and injured, the robber started to back out of the booth. No customers were around. As the workers pushed the man out, they got stabbed several more times. Fortunately for the workers, the blade wasn't large; it was smaller, about the size of a pocket knife. The robber, after taking several blows to the head and grabbing whatever money was on the counter, took off. The workers were hurt bad. One had a slice across his throat, several stab wounds, and was bleeding heavily. The other had been stabbed as well and was also a bloody mess. They managed to call the police who in turn called my mom at the house.

"How are they?" I asked as Mom put the pile of toast and eggs on the table.

"The cut on Mr. [Unnamed's] neck wasn't deep," she said. "He was very lucky."

The workers, though wounded severely, survived the attack. The lifesaving factor was that the knife was small. When Mom and Albert got to the station the night of the stabbing, there was blood all over the cashier's booth.

"It was disgusting," Albert recalled.

They wiped up the pools and streaks of blood; smears of it covered the cashier's booth door. Red handprints marked the spots where the workers had braced themselves during the struggle. The candy and soda on the countertops had splatters of blood on them and had to be thrown out. Mom and Albert cleaned up every speck and ounce of evidence from the fight and made sure the booth was pristine and ready for customers and another shift.

Although shaken by the incident, Mom gathered her courage and took over the rest of the shift with Albert. They worked the graveyard till 6 AM. Mom was sad. She wanted to go with the two workers to the hospital, but there was no one to take the rest of the shift. It was late at night, probably around 1 or 2 AM, when things finally calmed down and the police left.

I'm glad it wasn't us, I thought.

After the stabbing, the workers quit and Mom had to hire new employees to fill their spots. The positions were filled quickly, and Mom and I didn't have to pick up the extra hours; I was grateful. When she and I went to work the weekend after the stabbing, I was scared out of my mind. When she parked the car around 5:45 AM, Saturday morning, I told her to make sure no one was around before she got out.

"We need to be careful," I said. "I'll walk behind you and you go first."

"Don't be so scared," Mom said as she opened the car door. "It's not good."

I followed her as she walked toward the booth and made sure to look over my shoulder several times. As we neared the door, I inspected every dark corner and made sure there wasn't anyone on the sidewalk waiting to run in after us. I stared for a moment at the bus bench anchored on the sidewalk of Rosecrans to see if there was anyone lying down on it; nobody was there. The streets were empty. It was nearly 6 AM, and nobody was out. Mom unlocked the door, and we went inside.

I walked into the booth and stared at the inventory. Just a few days prior, everything was covered in blood. I couldn't imagine trying to do what the workers did. If it had been me, I would have surely died. I had no idea how to defend myself or fight back the way the workers did. But for now, in the booth, with the doors closed and locked, we were relatively safe. I sat down on my little blue cushioned chair as I helped Mom open the new shift.

My brothers and I didn't often work together at the station. But when we did, we'd chat and talk about school and things like the stabbing. We talked about the station and how much we hated being there because of the racism, the fights, and the crazy stuff we witnessed.

"What's the worst thing you've seen?" I asked Albert one evening at the station.

"I don't know," he said. "There's too many."

We'd seen countless drive-by shootings, stabbings, accidents, and what not since we started working. The rival station across the street almost always had an incident. They didn't have an enclosed cashier's booth like we did, and they sold alcohol. The other gas station's minimart was constantly being robbed. I was grateful for my little booth, its solid rock bottom and bulletproof windows.

"What about you?" Albert asked. "What's the craziest thing you've seen?

I thought for a moment.

"Besides all the racism?" I asked. "And the random shootings and stabbings?"

"Yeah," he said.

I went through the list of things in my head that I'd seen during the graveyard shifts. There had been several arguments with customers, several funny moments with high or drunk people, and just random, odd stuff like that one time some guy hit on me and asked why I didn't like chocolate.

"There was this one time when I was working with Mom in the morning, it was like 10 AM," I said. "Mom went to the back in the garage. We weren't too busy, so I was looking around at the pumps."

Albert adjusted his thick glasses and picked up a candy bar as he listened to my story.

"I heard this screeching sound, and when I turned to look, there was this car coming down Rosecrans really, really fast."

My brother nodded his head as he chewed on the chocolate and peanuts. *That looks good*, I thought as I grabbed one.

"Before I knew it," I said with my mouth full, "I saw this car spinning out of control and heading straight toward the other station!"

"No way," my brother said.

"Yup, the car spun out and hit the front pump over there," I said pointing across the street. "When the car hit, it just went POOF! The sides popped out and then it kind of caved in."

"Did it catch fire?" Albert asked.

"No," I said. "There was a little smoke. Nothing really happened. The driver got out. He seemed okay."

"Man," Albert said. "That's lucky."

Lucky indeed! The pump should have exploded. I should have seen a small mushroom cloud of smoke and fire; there should have been death and carnage! But, the employee at the other station had the good sense to turn off the gas with the emergency stop button; he saved a lot of lives. I wondered for a brief moment if he had the same big red emergency button I did.

Albert and I had similar stories to tell. Turns out we experienced a lot of the same stuff. We talked through the night. We compared notes on the fights we had and the crazy stuff we saw. We also realized we had similar experiences when it came to the racial tension. Only Albert got it worse than I did because he's a boy.

"So what do they say to you?" I asked as we opened a couple of sodas. I liked the grape-flavored ones, and he liked the cola.

"If it was a bad fight, they'd threaten to come back and shoot me."

I sipped my drink and let the carbonation linger on my tongue as I listened; I liked the bubbly feeling.

"Has anyone ever tried anything? Anyone ever come back like they said they would?" I asked.

"Nah," Albert said. "Our fights weren't bad enough for them to actually try and kill me."

"I get called a chink a lot," I said.

"Me too," he said.

"It's good we have the bulletproof glass." I added.

Chapter 5

"Something's Rotten in the State of Denmark" – Hamlet, William Shakespeare

When Dad died, I didn't understand it. Instead, I did my best to help Mom. I worried about her when I was at school, wondering if someone had finally made good on a threat. During those first few years at the gas station, we didn't know that the anger and resentment we felt from the people in the area were a result of a long history of government neglect and police brutality. I had no clue that the lack of educational and economic opportunities added to the racial conflict and unrest the black community felt. Coupled with the recession of the early 1990s, the rise in drug use, and gang violence, the area was a tinderbox. People were disgruntled, dismayed, and ready to rise up. I was angry and ignorant of these facts, sitting there in my bulletproof cashier's booth, wondering why I was a damn gook, and wondering what my Korean face had to do with the price of gas and cigarettes.

The Black-Korean Conflict made conditions worse in Compton and other inner cities throughout the United States. Blacks hated Koreans like me and Mom because we took jobs, we were rude, we sold inferior products, etc. Korean shop owners weren't big box retailers who could afford to buy in bulk from larger companies. Instead, Koreans bought from warehouses and sold those products. It was a lack of communication, cultural misunderstandings, and the whole shit ton of discrimination, neglect, and racism both our communities suffered, that created the gap between our two ethnicities. Historically, the problems that plagued South Central Los Angeles in the 1980s and 1990s were the same as the ones in the 1960s. Police brutality, poverty, lack of opportunities, and the overt racial discrimination and neglect by the government sparked the 1965 Watts Riots. The same issues persist to this day: the Ferguson Unrest (2014); the Baltimore Uprising (2015); the Charlotte, North Carolina Riots (2016); and so on and on. The Watts Riots claimed the lives of thirty-five people. Rioters burned down more than six hundred buildings. The incident began after the arrest of Marquette Frye, an African American man who had been pulled over for allegedly driving drunk. Frye's mother intervened. Frye's brother also tried to help, arguing with police officers.

Frye, his mom, and his brother were arrested. A crowd had begun to gather as the altercation between family and law enforcement played out. People threw things at the cops. The situation intensified. A riot broke out and lasted for six days. The National Guard had to be called in to help quell the violence.[9] Fast forward to 1992 and the same problems persisted. Police brutality and violence continued to plague the area.[10]

One of the first examples of police brutality to be caught on tape happened on March 3, 1991.[11] It involved Rodney King and the Los Angeles Police Department. In the case of King, he led police on a chase through the streets of LA. When it was over, King was surrounded by cops who beat him with their batons so severely that he was taken to a hospital. The media played the footage repeatedly. I was shocked by the images. I'd heard about police brutality from customers. I'd seen police abuse their power. But never had I seen cops beat someone like that.

The tape made headlines. The constant onslaught of the repeating footage on every news channel aroused people's sense of injustice. (Today, police brutality is still an issue. The "Black Lives Matter" movement is proof of that). Then to make matters worse, another incident was caught on camera on March 16, 1991, just two weeks after the King beating. This time it involved a Korean store owner and a young black girl.

"Mom, did you see the news?" I yelled as I ran up the stairs to her room one day after school. "A Korean lady shot a fifteen-year-old black girl and killed her!"

"What?" she asked.

"Turn on the TV," I said.

I sat next to her on her queen-sized bed. Pictures of a woman named Soon Ja Du flashed across the screen as a voiceover of a reporter narrated the story: Du had accused a young black girl, Latasha Harlins, of trying to shoplift a bottle of orange juice. The two argued. Du looked frazzled. Tired. Stressed. She looked like most of the Korean shop owners Mom and I knew. As the argument progressed, Du pulled Harlins' sweater as she approached the counter; they struggled. Harlins struck Du in the face. Du fell. Harlins "tossed" the juice on the counter, and walked out. Du grabbed a .38 caliber revolver from under the counter.

BANG!

Du shot Harlins in the back of the head.[12]

"Oh my god," I said to Mom. "It's just getting worse!"

Mom shook her head.

"This is bad," I said. "Mom, we really got to think about getting a gun. You never know who wants revenge."

"No," Mom said. "Stop thinking like that."

"But you saw what happened, that lady shot and killed that kid! People already don't like Koreans. It's just getting crazier! We've got to make sure we can defend ourselves."

"If you think getting a gun is going to make things better, you're not using your brain," she said as she got up.

"Then what do we do? When we go to the station, people are going to say stuff to us; blame us. What if they try to hurt us?"

"Don't worry about things like that," Mom said. "That didn't happen in Compton. Don't cause problems. Be nice. Be courteous. No one will try to hurt us if we don't stir up trouble. If you think having a gun is not going to cause problems for us, you're wrong."

"Yeah right," I called after her as she walked downstairs. "Sure."

The next weekend I worked, I was nervous and on the defensive. What was going on in the world? First the King beating, then the Latasha Harlins shooting. What next?

"Hey kid, when did the prices go up?" a black man asked one night.

"Last week," I said.

"You want me to pay $3.25? Man, I ain't made outta money. I can get these smokes cheaper at the store. Why you sellin' them for so much more?"

"So go over there," I said. "This is a gas station, not a grocery store."

"Stupid kid, if I wanted to go to the store, I'd be there. How come you chinks always rip us off? Comin' in the hood where you don't belong."

"Look, man, want them or not?"

"Bitch," he said.

"$3.25," I said.

He slammed his money down and I gave him the cigarettes.

"Chink, go back to where you came from."

As tension continued to simmer, Korean shop owners became the target of protests, armed robberies, beatings, thefts, and all manner of criminal activity. Many Koreans lost their lives trying to live the American dream. Meanwhile, in Los Angeles, industries relocated, plants closed, and foreign investment took over. The economic restructuring, coupled with the demographic shift, only added fuel to the racial and class inequality conflict.

The 1987 Black Monday stock market crash kicked off the economic woes of the nation. As the joblessness continued, the economy sank. By 1991, the country was knee-deep in recession. The unemployment rate reached 7.5 percent by 1992.[13] I felt the racism surge as I worked with Mom during those tumultuous years of economic struggle. As we watched the growing tally of Korean deaths, heard about shootings of Mom's liquor store owner acquaintances, learned about the robberies that nearly took the lives or did take the lives of other family acquaintances, we were alarmed. I was terrified.

Nothing I learned in school prepared me for the type of racism and violence I witnessed. Nothing at all. I couldn't talk to Mr. Smith, to my favorite teacher Mrs. Archie, or any other person at school about the fear I felt every time I walked from the car to the booth on Saturday mornings. I couldn't tell them about the tension between blacks and Koreans and how it bothered me so much that sometimes I dreamed about it.

The strife between Koreans and African Americans was like a taut drum, the membrane stretched so tight, it was about to snap. At some point, there was even a center that sought to mediate relations between blacks and Koreans. The Asian Pacific American Dispute Resolution Center (APADRC) tried to give voice to the Korean community. Leaders from Korean organizations spoke out in newspapers, including the *Los Angeles Times*, about the growing concern over potential violence.

"As a Korean-American, I am afraid when people say they are going to take this to the streets," said Marcia Choo, director of the APADRC in a November 17, 1991 *LA Times* article. "All it takes is just one person to break down everything we've worked for."

As overall homicides in Compton rose – eighty-four by 1989 – and conflicts between Koreans and blacks intensified, journalist K.W. Lee provided a Korean American insider perspective when he started publishing the English edition of *The Korea Times* in 1990. Lee – the godfather of Asian American journalism – published numerous stories about the racial conflict and the resulting violence. In fact, the publication had an Op-Ed exchange program with the African American newspaper the *Sentinel*, which was based in Los Angeles. Mom never knew about the paper, and it wasn't until I was in graduate school that I found out about it. If only people would have listened then. If only we listened now.

While all this racism was going on in the 1980s, Mom and Dad tried to keep out of it. Mom tried to be even more inconspicuous after Dad died. She just worked and kept her head low. She tried to avoid the gangs, criminal activities, and general lawlessness that seemed to rule the area. She hoped that the racism wouldn't affect her or me. But it did. The Black-Korean Conflict was at our doorstep by the early 1990s. The cultural misunderstandings and racism ran so deep, a group of organizations formed the Black Korean Alliance (BKA). Founded in the spring of 1986, the group worked to improve relations between Korean and African Americans. One of the BKA's activities included a "Korean-African American Friendship Cultural Festival" held in the late 1980s. The event was supposed to celebrate the "Day of Korean and African American Community" that was declared by the city of Compton on March 9, 1985. A large turnout was expected. Organizers said two thousand African Americans and one thousand Koreans would attend. Only one hundred African Americans and eight hundred Koreans showed up.[14] My parents were not there.

By the 1990s, when I was working with Mom, the lack of coverage about Korean shop owners being robbed, hurt, or shot and killed, made us feel alienated. We were constantly reading stories in the news about Koreans shooting African Americans. Yet we heard little of the ten Koreans who were robbed and killed in Los Angeles in 1991 alone. Instead, the media reported on the tension and conflict between our two ethnicities. We felt vilified.

In the same year of the shooting of Latasha Harlins, a Korean business owner was shot and killed during a robbery at his store in Southwest Los Angeles. Another Korean-owned store was burned. Meanwhile, two blacks were killed by Koreans.[15] The problems between the communities was palpable. So, when three months after the Latasha Harlins shooting in 1991, Lee Arthur Mitchel was shot and killed by Tae Sam Park, I could almost taste the gunpowder in the air.

Tae Sam Park was the owner of John's Market in South Central Los Angeles. Park was defending himself and his wife when he shot Mitchel, according to news reports. Police concluded that Park was acting in self-defense. But the black community didn't see it that way, and they boycotted his store for months, adding to the mix of frustrations.[16] The fights between myself and customers continued to be racially charged. We cussed at each other like scurvy-ridden sailors, stuck in the middle of nowhere with no one else to blame but each other. I felt the conflict rising. I could feel the hatred toward Koreans with every "gook" comment I got. The threats replayed in my head like my worn-out Paula Abdul tape. I really, really wanted Mom to get a gun. She wouldn't give in, though I begged and begged.

"These black guys are going to come here and shoot you or me," I said one night during a graveyard shift at the station. "They don't care about age. They don't care about the fact that I'm just a kid. I don't want to die here in this shithole!"

"Stop it," Mom said. "Go back to the booth. Don't cuss!"

"I hate it here," I yelled.

"If you don't go back to the booth right now…"

"Mom!"

"You listen," she said as she started to stand up. I was in the hallway, she was in the office sitting down, trying to enjoy a meal. "If you keep saying those stupid things and thinking those thoughts, you're going to end up getting hurt. Do you want that?"

"No, but what I'm saying is true! We need a gun!"

"We don't," she said as she started to walk toward me.

"Come on!" I said. "Something bad is going to happen to us someday and we won't be prepared!"

"Go to the office," she said. "Eat something."

She never gave in to my demands for a gun.

Chapter 6

Los Angeles on Fire

April 29, 1992 – or *Sa-i-gu* as Koreans call it – started out like any other school day for me and my brothers. (*Sa-i-gu* literally translates to 4-29 in Korean.) That morning I woke up and got dressed in a skirt and shirt. Mom dropped me and my brothers off and went to the station. I had just turned twelve years old and was about to finish the sixth grade.

It was a Wednesday, and the teachers had just hit their midweek stride in their lesson plans. I went through the usual routine; I made it through the classes. I ate my lunch with my friends. I thought about the looming work weekend that lay ahead. After school, my brothers and I walked home. Mom had to work late that day.

Tony went into the den and turned on the old tube television we had since I was born; it was made with wood encasing and a glass face; it had bulky knobs we had to turn with force to change the channels. I went upstairs and put my blue backpack in my room and went to the bathroom. When I finally joined my brother in the den, he was watching the news. I sat down next to him on the brown carpet. We often watched television sitting on the floor of the den; it was our playroom where we kept toys and videogames. Mom kept a pile of laundry in the corner; one sliding glass door led to the backyard on one side and another big wood door led to the garage on the other side. Next to the garage door is a small bathroom that I hated to use because it was so small and sometimes, it smelled.

"Why are you watching this?" I asked Tony. "Turn on the cartoons."

"The Rodney King verdict was not guilty," Tony said.

"Wow," I said. "I wonder what's going to happen now."

The verdicts were the culmination of a yearlong investigation into the Rodney King beating. King was driving his white 1988 sedan on March 3, 1991, when two California Highway Patrol officers began following his car. He was with two friends. King led the officers on a high-speed chase. Eventually, King pulled over on Foothill Boulevard, which is located in Lake View Terrace, California. Police removed King from his car and subdued him with batons and Taser guns. That's when George Holliday, a manager at a plumbing and rooting company living at a nearby apartment complex, started filming the incident on his video camera. The video, which was lit by police car's headlights and by street lamps, shows King being beaten by the cops, who stood around him in a circle for several minutes, kicking and hitting him. King was struck more than fifty times with batons. He was later sent to a hospital with multiple cuts and fractures, according to news reports.[17]

By March 4, 1991, the video spread like wildfire and was aired on local news stations and on commercial media networks nationwide. Then on March 15, 1991, Sergeant Stacey Koon, Officers Laurence Powell, Theodore Briseno, and Timothy Wind, were arraigned on charges of excessive force and assault with a deadly weapon during the King arrest.

On November 26, 1991, lawyers for the defense were granted a change of venue for the trial; it was moved from Los Angeles County to Simi Valley in Ventura County. By March 4, 1992, the trial began. Eighty-one seconds of the video were used as evidence. The video was shown in varying speeds: slow motion, super slow motion, and normal. The prosecutor told the jury that after watching the tape and hearing testimony, each one would find himself saying, "Enough is enough."[18]

The defense countered, saying that the officers were doing their jobs.[19] The defense kept using "the thin blue line" as their catchphrase, meaning that the role of police was to protect society.

As the trial dragged on, people at the gas station talked about the case, voicing their concerns. "No justice, no peace." "Them cops are guilty." "King shouldn't have been beaten." Mom didn't say much to me about the case, but I followed it nonetheless. I was fascinated by the details. As much as I despised my racist customers, I knew that what happened to King was wrong.

The jury, which consisted of ten Caucasians, one Hispanic, and one Filipino-American, acquitted the four officers on April 29, 1992. The acquittal caused an upheaval and politicians and community activists voiced their concerns. Even Bill Clinton, who was the governor of Arkansas at the time, said that what he saw on the tape looked "excessive" to him.[20]

The video and the resulting verdicts ignited public outrage over police brutality. The trial shined a light on the socio-economic inequalities and racial tension in Los Angeles that we'd been watching brew for years. Shortly after the verdicts were announced, Los Angeles Mayor Tom Bradley and Police Chief Daryl Gates held a press conference.

Gates appealed to the masses for calm and stated that the system had failed.[21] I wasn't sure what was going to happen. As Tony and I watched coverage of the acquittal and the various experts that talked about what it all meant, news reports began to emerge about concerned citizens gathering to protest. The reports started to pour in: a crowd of three hundred gathered outside the Simi Valley Courthouse where the trial took place. City leaders asked for people to remain "calm." But, how could they? How could I?

"I'm going to call Mom," Albert said. He had joined me and Tony in the den.

Mom was still at the gas station, working a shift with Mr. Chung, one of her employees. I was glad I wasn't there. Albert went to the kitchen. I followed him. He picked up the phone. The long, curly, yellow cord connecting the receiver to the base dangled as he dialed the number to the booth.

"Did you hear?" he asked Mom. "The verdict was not guilty."

"That's unfortunate," Mom said to him. "Did you guys eat something? There's some food in the refrigerator. I'll be home by six."

She hadn't grasped the gravity of the situation. Albert told her to come as soon as she could, he didn't like what was being shown on the news: people gathering in large numbers in South Central Los Angeles, people carrying signs and protesting for justice. But Mom told him to not worry.

Around 4 PM, a group of people went to Florence and Normandie Avenues in South Central LA to protest. I watched the crowd yelling and screaming at the cameramen and the police that had shown up to keep the peace. I wrung my hands. The area where the protesters were was about eleven minutes away from Mom's place.

Albert called Mom again and told her what was happening. As we watched the situation escalate, I shook my head in disbelief as the news reported that the police were dispatched to Florence and Normandie Avenues but were recalled. They didn't come back for about three hours.[22]

Back at the station, Mom was standing inside the cashier's booth with Mr. Chung. They watched as a large number of African Americans got together and stood under the gas station's price sign. Mom was confused. The people were yelling at passing cars. Some even threw cans. Scared, she decided to stay inside the booth with Mr. Chung. Mom saw more and more people gathering on the streets. Many of them had bats, cardboard signs, bottles, and other things in their hands.

"Mom," Albert said to her over the phone around 5 PM. "The news says there's lots of people protesting near the station, just a few miles away. You got to come home."

I sat at the kitchen table with my brother as he talked to Mom. I wanted to talk to her. Maybe she would listen to me? But Albert hung up before I got a chance to say anything.

At the station, the crowd of people at the corner got rowdier. As the minutes progressed, customers kept pulling in for gas; it was like a stampede of water-starved horses. Mom could do nothing but stay in the bulletproof cashier's booth with Mr. Chung. People filled up their tanks, ignoring the click of the topping over sound the nozzles made when the gas tanks were full. People drove off and came back with jugs and other containers and filled those up too. Some came back with their spouses' cars. Some looked worried. Some looked excited. Some yelled and cussed at Mom and Mr. Chung.

"Why's the gas so expensive?!" one person yelled as he dropped a few bucks into the tray.

Mom picked up the bills.

"What number, please?" she said as politely as she could.

As she stood there, avoiding direct eye contact with the customer, she kept her head slightly bowed until the customer finally said, "Number nine."

Mom tried not to do anything that might provoke the customers or the group of people that were gathered under the price sign. She and Mr. Chung just worked and kept their demeanor as submissive as possible. At this point, they knew they were in trouble.

At home, my brothers and I were glued to the television. We couldn't believe what was happening. I was worried about Mom. *Had she remembered to lock the side door? Did she remember to hide the money bags under the register? Did she park her car near the garage?* Albert and Tony kept calling Mom, urging her to leave, telling her about the growing protests that were turning violent.

"I can't," she said nervously to Albert on the phone. "There are too many people outside."

"Just leave," Albert said. "Just go to the car as fast as you can and get out of there!"

Around 6:45 p.m. the news started to roll footage of a man – Reginald

Denny – being attacked by a group of African Americans on Normandie Avenue in Los Angeles. Protestors dragged Denny out of his truck and beat him badly. He nearly died.[23]

"Where's the police?!" I asked to no one in particular as I stared at the television. "This is crazy!"

Footage of stores being looted and burned, and well, straight-up rioting, dominated the channels. Dumbfounded at the stupidity of the situation, I could do nothing as I watched. Then, just a few minutes after the Reginald Denny incident, another man – Fidel Lopez – was beaten. The violence escalated. Cameras caught scenes of the chaos: fires, looting, and the madness that riots encourage. One of the first businesses to be looted was Tom's Liquor and Deli at the intersection of Florence and Normandie Avenues. At some point, I couldn't watch anymore. I got up and went to the phone in the kitchen; it was my turn to try and convince Mom to come home.

"Mom!" I yelled when she picked up. "People are rioting! You're going to get hurt! Get out of there!"

"I'm trying," she said as calmly as she could. "I have to go now."

She hung up.

Worried, I could do nothing but pester my brothers and watch television. *How could people do this to their own neighborhoods?* I thought.

Mom was beside herself trying to understand what was happening, she later told me. Throughout the day, neighborhood people kept telling her to leave.

"You gotta get outta here," one long-time customer told Mom. "Things are gonna get bad. We don't know what's gonna happen."

"People are saying there might be trouble," another customer said to her. "We don't know if you're going to get hurt; you really need to leave, Mrs. Park!"

The problem was, she couldn't exactly just saunter out of there. No one would escort her or Mr. Chung out of the booth. People were looking out for themselves and rightfully so. The police were nowhere to be found. Mom tried calling several times for help. No one ever came. Finally, Mom took matters into her own hands. She decided she and Mr. Chung would have to make a break for it on their own. Outside, people were running around on the streets with bats, bottles, sticks, cans, and rocks. They were shouting and throwing stuff at cars.

By this point, Mom and Mr. Chung had sold almost 9,000 gallons of gas, which was worth more than $10,000 at the time. There was only a little bit of gas left in the tanks. Mom decided to start turning people away. She knew she had to take the cash. But the mob of people at the corner of the station worried her. She devised a plan.

Mom grabbed a blue water bucket and put all the money inside. Mr. Chung kept watch and made sure there was no one at the windows. If someone came by, they acted like they were cleaning. Mom tried to pass the bucket off as a trashcan and put random bits of garbage over the cash: empty cigarette cartons, paper towels, rags, and crushed soda cans. How many times had she and I just thrown out that rubbish? This time, it was more than just trash; it was a lifesaving accomplice.

"We have no more gas," she told people as they came to the window. "The company won't deliver here right now. We have nothing."

"Come on!" customers complained. "Turn on the pumps!"

"There's nothing," Mom said, knowing she had to lie or she would never be able to leave.

Eventually, people believed her, and the flow of customers died down. At home, Tony, Albert, and I were outraged at what we were watching; people yelling and screaming, burning buildings down, people getting beaten, police nowhere in sight, and cities in complete turmoil. We called Mom again.

"Two guys were just beaten up," Albert said to her.

We were in the kitchen, gathered around the phone as Albert updated Mom on the ever-growing violence. Stressed, I tapped my fingers on the brown table. I felt like I was in the booth; impatient, anxious, worried, annoyed, angry. I forgot to wash the rice for dinner.

"I'll come when I can. Stop calling," Mom said to Albert. "I have to go."

"Is she coming?" I asked him as he hung up the phone.

"She says she is."

A little past 7:30 PM, Mom and Mr. Chung decided to take a chance and leave the gas station. The police weren't coming, and it was up to them to get out of there safely. They braced themselves as they got ready to go outside and head for their cars.

Very calmly and as inconspicuously as possible, they opened the side door. Mom and Mr. Chung walked out of the cashier's booth with the blue bucket filled with thousands of dollars in rubber banded hundreds, twenties, tens, fives, and single dollar bills. Mr. Chung held one side of it, while Mom held the other, trying to make it look like it was just trash they were going to throw away in the dumpster.

Most of the people under the price sign didn't notice them, and those that did chose to ignore them. No one paid them any attention as they walked the seventy-five feet or so toward their respective cars. Mom took the bucket from Mr. Chung when they got to her car. Mr. Chung went to his vehicle. Mom opened the passenger's door of her car, behind the driver, and set the bucket down inside. Some of the people from the neighborhood walked by; they said nothing to her as she got into the driver's seat. I was glad the Benz was built like a tank. If anyone tried to shoot at it or hit it with something, it could withstand the attack long enough for Mom to get the hell out of there.

Meanwhile, Mr. Chung started his car and was waiting for Mom to back hers out. Mom turned the ignition on, closed her door, gripped the steering wheel, and put the car in reverse. She backed out slowly. People continued to ignore her. Mr. Chung pulled up behind her. Mom drove the couple of feet to the exit, flipped her ticker on, looked once to the left, and then drove out onto Rosecrans. Mr. Chung followed her lead.

Mom drove down the little stretch of street that led to the 710 freeway entrance and to safety without trouble. Mr. Chung and Mom didn't get beaten or dragged out of their cars like Reginald Denny or Fidel Lopez. When Mom came home, my brothers and I ran to the door to greet her.

"Did anyone follow you?" Albert asked. "What happened to Mr. Chung? No one tried to hurt you, right?"

"How did you get away?" Tony asked. "What's in that blue bucket?"

"Did people try to break into the booth?" I asked.

She tried to shoo us away as we trailed alongside her.

"Go do your homework, stop worrying," she said in Korean as she took off her shoes. "Everything is fine."

She put the blue bucket she was carrying down in her makeshift office in the living room and walked to the kitchen. I followed her in as my brothers went back to the den to watch more news. Mom opened the refrigerator and grabbed some food. She made herself some dinner because I forgot to wash the rice and cook; I was too busy watching the news and the escalating violence in Los Angeles. I sat down at the table and bombarded her with more questions.

"Did people yell at you?" I asked. "The TV said people were burning things down and looting. Did they try to do that at the station?"

Mom put her plate of cold Korean side dishes – spinach, bean sprouts, and soy sauce boiled beef – on the table. She shook her head no to my questions and sat down. She ate like nothing had happened.

More than sixty people died because of the riots.[24] Innocent bystanders were beaten. *Sa-i-gu* devastated the Korean American community, the African American community, and really our whole society. When the Los Angeles Riots broke out, the six days of civil unrest held no justice for me. Racially motivated people looted, burned, and murdered.

How could people do this to each other? I thought as I watched news coverage of the violence. *It's unbelievable.*

Throughout the first day of the riots, cities began to shut down. The Rapid Transit District stopped servicing South Central Los Angeles. Rioting was visible from the Hollywood Hills to the city of Long Beach.[25]

The second day of the riots, April 30, was a Thursday. My brothers and I went to school, and this time, my day was far from routine. I worried about Mom. Would she try to go to the gas station? Some of the teachers at school asked me about her.

"How's everything?" the principal's wife asked. "How's your mom and your business? We're praying for everyone over there."

I shrugged my shoulders. What was prayer going to do against a mob of angry people? What was prayer going to do against a Molotov cocktail or guns? We needed more than prayers. My friend Natalie – the one who lived in Compton – said little about what was going on. Once she asked me if my family was okay, and I told her we were fine so far.

"Stay safe," I told her.

When my brothers and I got home from school that day, Mom was sitting in her room. She had stayed home because Mayor Tom Bradley declared a state of emergency. I was relieved to see her. She was watching the news. That night, we watched Korean and American reports about the riots. At some point, President George H.W. Bush spoke out for peace. My family listened as he appealed for reason and asked for calm.

"The court system has worked," President Bush said. "What's needed now is calm, respect for the law."[26]

His words fell on deaf ears. The night wore on. Scenes of burning buildings, bloodied bystanders and rioters, looters and gun fights flashed across the screen nonstop. I was disturbed by what I was seeing. Sitting there in my school's physical education class outfit – blue shorts and a white t-shirt – I scratched my head in bewilderment as one thought kept running through my head:

People are crazy!

"Look carefully and see if they show Compton," Mom said as we watched. "Maybe we can see if the station is still there."

We kept our eyes glued to the television. Suddenly, I had an idea.

"Mom, how about I call Natalie and ask if she can see the station from her house?" I said. "She lives pretty close by and her dad has that church. Maybe she can see it from there?"

Mom's eyebrows arched in approval. I picked up the phone and twirled the cord around my finger as I dialed my friend's number.

"Hi Natalie," I said, surprised that she was the one to pick up the phone. "How are you guys doing?"

"We're okay," she said. "It's bad out there, though."

"Staying safe?"

"Yeah," she said.

"I'm sorry to bother you with this, but my mom is really worried about the station, and I thought maybe you could see it from your house; can you see it? Is it burning?"

"Hold on," she said. "Let me check."

She looked out of her window. A few moments later she got back on the phone.

"No, it's not on fire," she said. "It looks okay."

"Thank God," I said. "And thank you."

"No problem," Natalie said. "Call me back if you want in a few hours, and I'll tell you if it's still there."

"Thanks and be careful!" I said.

We were a couple of sixth graders learning the fear of adulthood.

During the riots, Mom read the Korean newspaper and listened to Radio Korea, which served as a call center for Koreans caught in the violence who couldn't rely on police for help.[27] She watched Korean television. She told us that Korean American business owners had organized their own defense. The police had clearly abandoned Koreatown, a city situated in the mid-Wilshire District of Los Angeles. We listened to reporters talk about Korean Americans fighting against looters and would-be arsonists.

One group called itself the Korean American Young Adult Team; the band of young Koreans formed taskforces that responded to calls for help from other Koreans and tried to help them protect their businesses.[28] I wished I was part of that group, working to protect the things our parents worked so hard for. But alas, I was just a kid.

A corner shopping center is fully engulfed in flames as it is left burning out of control in Koreatown, Los Angeles, California on May 1, 1992, the third day of the 1992 Los Angeles Riots. According to Professor Ed Chang of UC Riverside, 2,280 Korean American-owned stores were either totally destroyed, looted, or suffered loss with total damage of $400 million in the 1992 Los Angeles Riots.
Photo Courtesy Hyungwon Kang/Los Angeles Times

"Are you going to the station tomorrow?" Albert asked Mom as the television blared in the background. "You can't go!"

Mom didn't say anything and hushed him so we could keep watching. Gun battles straight out of an old western movie ensued. People Mom knew sat on their rooftops, rifles and guns in hand, trying to save what they had worked so long and hard to create.

"No," Mom answered Albert. "No, I can't. It's too dangerous. But if things get better, I'll try and go. I left so much inventory. We can't afford to lose everything."

Mom had left thousands of dollars of cigarettes, candy, soda, and other merchandise. She had also left thousands of dollars in shift money in the big steel safe. Mom fidgeted with her pillow as we continued watching the news. Footage of people ransacking businesses, taking shoes, clothes, and whatever else was around continued; on and on, for hours the footage rolled.

Riots breed looters; it's just a fact.

News reports of the chaos continued. I watched in horror. I watched as footage of Koreans defending their businesses flashed across the screen. If Dad had been alive, he would have been out there, too. Commentators and know-it-alls started to appear on TV, pointing their fingers at the Black-Korean Conflict and the not-guilty verdicts as the main reasons for the uprising.

How horribly wrong they were, I realized years later. It was more than that, it was the neglect and the poverty that persisted since the days of the 1965 Watts Riots. It was the frustrations of the crime-ridden communities, the dejectedness of the poorly educated because no one wanted to teach there and because it seemed that no one really cared. It was the sadness due to the deaths and murders of people by gangs, cops and random criminals; it was the hopelessness of the drug addicted who couldn't escape the vicious cycle of highs and lows and all the things in between. Yet people turned a blind eye to the messed-up lives of the destitute in those worn-out towns and cities that needed more than just peace banners. The despair and frustrations that plagued the communities of South Central Los Angeles before the riots had a lot more to do with those factors than just racism.

When customers yelled at me because the cost of gas was too high or cigarette prices went up again, it wasn't my ethnicity they were singling out. I realized, years later, that it was the whole kit and caboodle; it was a social and economic problem, not just a racial one. Before the riots broke out, I sensed that dejectedness but didn't fully understand it till much later.

"It's not our fault the gas prices are higher," I yelled one late Saturday evening, just a few weeks before the riots. "Ask the company why they're raising the cost. We only make a few pennies a gallon as it is."

"Then why's it cheaper a few streets down?!" the female customer asked.

"By what? A penny?" I said. "That's not a big difference. You don't like it? Go over there."

"Dumb chinks think we're made out of money or something?" the woman said. "It's hard enough tryin' to pay my bills!"

She threw a couple of dollars into the tray.

"It's not my fault things are all messed up," I said. "We're not 'ripping' you off."

As she was about to walk away, the woman slapped the window with her hand and cussed at me.

When Friday, May 1, 1992 – the third day of the riots – dawned, Mom fretted. For Koreans, help was absent. Koreatown looked like a war zone. Hundreds of buildings had been burned down. Looters had wreaked havoc overnight. Smoke filled the skies of Los Angeles County. Rioters and looters swarmed on businesses like ants, hunting for the best product, the best prize. *This was all so wrong, so terribly wrong*, I thought. *Where were the police?*

Armed volunteers guard California market from the roof in Koreatown, Los Angeles, California on May 1, 1992, on the third day of the 1992 Los Angeles Riots. According to Professor Ed Chang of UC Riverside, 2,280 Korean American-owned stores were either totally destroyed, looted, or suffered loss with total damage of $400 million in the 1992 Los Angeles Riots.
Photo Courtesy Hyungwon Kang/Los Angeles Times

Mom was beside herself with concern. Had the station been burned? My friend Natalie had kept us updated on what she could see from her window, but Mom wanted to see for herself if the station was still standing. That day, Mayor Bradley announced that gas could only be sold for use in cars. (Too many rioters had used gas for Molotov cocktails and burned down buildings with them). For Mom, it made no difference; she had already shut down on the first day. Plus, the company refused to deliver to the violence-ridden cities. Officials had also announced that morning that up to 4,000 federal troops were being sent to Los Angeles.[29]

Korean Americans organized a "peace rally" in Koreatown. They gathered and marched for calm, calling for an end to the rioting and destruction. The rally became the largest gathering of Asian Americans in the United States at the time. For Korean Americans, this was the moment to speak up. Korean Americans needed to stand up and become visible, so they did. The loss of years of work and of dreams shattered many Korean American lives. *Damn riots*, I thought that night as I lay in my bed.

For me and my brothers, May 1 was another day at school. I could barely handle it. Mom made breakfast for us that morning like usual. The only difference was that she didn't have to go to work. She hadn't had a day off since Dad died, but she couldn't enjoy the rare moment because she was so concerned about the station. As we sat around the table, I worried about Mom. *Is she going to try to go to the station?*

"What will you do?" Tony asked her as if he read my mind.

"Don't go to the station," Albert said.

I didn't say anything. I just focused on my rice as my brothers tried to convince her to stay. Mom kept quiet. After we finished breakfast, she loaded us into the car and took us to school.

"Don't worry," she said to us as she drove away. "Be good today."

When she got home, Mom decided she needed to get to the station, she later recalled. She needed to see that the last bit of hope she had to keep me and my brothers fed, clothed, and well hadn't become a casualty of the riots. Were the bulletproof glass windows of the booth holding up against the tirade of rioters and looters?

Mom knew that she couldn't get to the station alone. She couldn't drive to Compton because the freeways and streets to the city were blocked off. Mom sat down on the three-seat gray couch in our living room. She wondered how she could get there. Frustrated, she went upstairs to her room and watched the news. As scenes of looting and burning flashed, she paced the floor, trying to think of a way to get to the station.

Meanwhile, at school, I couldn't focus on my work. *Is Mom at the station now? Are the cops going to be there? Did the rioters break into the booth? Did they shatter the bulletproof glass? Was it even possible to break those windows?* I wondered.

At home, Mom sat on her bed and thought about us, our futures, our lives. She looked out at the backyard of our neighbor's house from her window; it was green and lush. It was a pretty May Day morning. After a few moments, she picked up the phonebook on the nightstand and thumbed through it. She found the number she was looking for and dialed.

"Hello," she said in her Korean accent. "I need taxi please."

She gave the address, and the taxi showed up about half an hour later.

"I need go Compton," she said to the driver. "Can you going there?"

"The freeways are closed," the taxi driver said. "There's no access."

"Take me close?" Mom asked as she flashed him some money. "Maybe Bellflower?"

"All right," he said as he looked at the twenty-dollar bill. As Mom hopped into the backseat of the cab, the driver popped the trunk. He reached inside and pulled out a sawed-off shotgun.

"You never know what can happen," he said to Mom as he climbed into the driver's seat and set the gun down on the floor of the passenger's side. "Let's go."

They drove to the 605 South freeway entrance, connected to the 91 West and exited Atlantic Avenue, right before the 710 North interchange. Mom eyeballed the streets. She was in Paramount, just a couple of miles away from Compton. As she looked around, she saw that access to Compton via Atlantic Avenue was still blocked off. Cops were guarding the streets.

"Okay," Mom said to the driver. "Stop here."

The taxi cab had driven close to one of the police blockades. Mom got out and stepped onto the sidewalk. There were people milling around. Some businesses were open. Mom walked toward the cops, hoping they would help her. She was surprised by how quiet the area was.

At school, I watched the clock anxiously. I tapped my pencil on my desk. I wondered where Mom was, and I waited for the bell to ring. I wanted to get home as fast as I could and see if Mom had really gone to the station; she certainly had the gall to do it!

Maybe I should pretend to be sick? Maybe I can make up something and say I need to call Mom? Maybe...

I understood her concern. I felt her distress when the riots broke out. How many hours had she and I spent in that little booth? We had invested so much of our lives working there, putting up with the long hours and the harassment. I prayed that the booth was still standing, despite my deep resentment for it. What would we do without it? I had come to hate and love my little box.

Mom walked toward the cops and waved her hands at them; either they didn't see her or they just chose to ignore her. She waved again, but this time she caught the attention of a cop car that was driving by. Before she made it to the blockade, the cop car pulled over and asked if she was okay.

"I need go my business in Compton," she said in her Korean accent. "It close. Need seeing if still there."

The cops looked tired.

"Please," she continued. "It only thing I having. Please helping me?"

The two male cops finally agreed to take her.

"Get in," one of them said.

Mom got into the rear seat, and they drove off to the station. She worried about what she would see. A pile of rubble perhaps? The police cruiser pulled up to the station on Atlantic. Mom got out. The station was intact. She felt safe; the cops stuck around and National Guard troops were visible on the streets. No rioters were in sight.

Mom walked around the station and inspected everything. The glass garage door had been broken. The garage bay doors had been smashed in. Looters had made off with tools, tires, oil, and other inventory Mom kept in the garage.

The booth was fine. No one had gotten in. Thank God for bulletproof glass windows and solid metal doors. Mom was relieved the damage wasn't worse. The station was still standing! She could replace the inventory. She could fix the doors. Mom was lucky. Across the street, the donut shop, the market – pretty much most of the complex – had been burned to a crisp. The blackened shell of those once-bustling businesses looked eerie in the morning light. Mom looked to see if Eggo might be there; he wasn't.

As she surveyed the area surrounding the station, she saw some troops standing on the sidewalk armed with guns. They looked tired, Mom recalled. The green of their uniforms clashed with the orange of the gas station's sign. Mom decided to approach them.

"Hello," she said.

"Good morning, ma'am," one of the troops said.

"How everything here?" she asked.

"Getting better," the soldier said. "Are you the owner of this gas station?"

"Yes," she said. "Can opening tomorrow?"

"No, ma'am, I'd say wait at least one more day," he said. "We're still gaining control of the situation, be careful. Go home."

Mom thanked the troops and went back to the cops, who were still waiting in their car for her.

"Can please taking me to Bellflower?" she asked them.

"Sure," they said as they motioned her to get in. After they dropped Mom off in Bellflower, she found a dingy looking payphone and called a taxi cab and went home. By 6 PM that day, 6,000 National Guard troops had been deployed.[30] The rioting had died down because of the presence of such heavy law enforcement. Troops ferreted out rioters, suppressed new threats, set up perimeters, and tried to restore peace as quickly as possible. As the evening wore on, an additional 4,000 soldiers and marines arrived.[31] They patrolled the burning streets in Humvees and Jeeps. I was relieved when I saw Mom coming to pick us up from school. She was safe! On the way home I blasted her with questions and she told me what she saw that day.

"How did you get there? Is the station still standing? Did they break into the booth? What did you see? Are people still rioting?"

"The booth is still there," Mom said in Korean. "Thank God."

"Was the station damaged at all?" Albert asked.

"Yes, they took a lot of the inventory," Mom said. "They broke the garage door, and it looks like they drove a car into the bay doors. They're smashed."

"At least they didn't burn it down," Tony chimed in. "What about the other station?"

"It's there," Mom said, "but they burned down the complex across the street."

Though I was stunned to hear the news, I was grateful it hadn't been us. That night, Mom slept a little bit better. Reports of violence had simmered down. Order was finally being restored. I was relieved that the booth was still standing. I should have been disappointed, but somewhere in all the craziness of the riots, something in me finally understood: we needed that damn business. That booth was my second home.

When May 2 dawned, the fourth day of the riots, Marines arrived in Los Angeles. As peace began to take shape, 30,000 people marched in a rally for racial healing.[32] Legions of volunteers took to the streets to help clean up and rebuild. That day was a Saturday, so the whole family stayed home. For once, Mom and I didn't have to go to work. What should have been a glorious Saturday afternoon for me and Mom was filled with worries. I actually wanted to be at the station. It was strange for me not to be tired on a Saturday. I was anxious all day.

"Mom, should I call my friend?" I asked her that afternoon.

"No," she said. "There were soldiers at the station yesterday."

We were sitting on her bed in her room. Mom turned on the television and surfed the channels. I told her to stop when I saw some news coverage of the riots. She turned it off.

"We don't need to watch that right now," she said. "Let's go downstairs and eat."

That night, I wondered if we would go to work the next day. *Could we open the first shift?* On Sunday, May 3, the Rapid Transit District bus system resumed service into South Central Los Angeles. The Reverend Jesse Jackson showed his concern for Koreans and met with leaders in Koreatown. He asked that the animosity between Koreans and African Americans would end. Reverend Jackson also prayed for victims and visited churches in the African American community. By 11:30 AM, Mayor Bradley announced that the dusk-to-dawn curfew would be lifted the next day.

Mom decided to reopen the station. The tanks still had about a thousand gallons of gas left. It was enough to at least get through one day. Besides, not many people were out on the streets. As peace took shape, pockets of violence still occurred, including the shooting of a Latino man who tried to run down National Guard troops with his car. The man died later that evening. But despite the incidents, normal life began to resume. Mom called the workers and asked if they would come back and open the new shift. One of them agreed. Mom felt confident that she could go meet the worker.

"I'll go to the station," she told us.

"We'll go with you," Albert said to her. "We can help."

"Yeah," I chimed in. "I want to come."

"No," she said. "Stay home."

"Mom, let me and Tony go. The news says it's safe now," Albert said firmly. "You're going to need our help, and I don't want you to go there by yourself again."

Mom looked at her second oldest son; the determination in his eyes convinced her.

"Okay," Mom said. "But Carol, you stay here."

"What?!" I said. "No way! I'm coming, too!"

"No," Mom said.

"Mom's right," Albert said. "We don't need you there."

"That's not fair," I said. "I want to go! You just said it was safe!"

Mom picked up her keys, and my brothers started to put their shoes on.

"Stay and clean the house," Mom said to me as they left. "That will be more helpful."

I knew I couldn't fight her on this one. My brothers weren't backing me up either. I had to give in. Mom and my brothers drove to the gas station without being turned around. The roads were open, and they saw troops patrolling here and there as they pulled up to the pumps. One of the workers had shown up and was in the booth. There were very few customers.

The scene was something they would never forget. The lack of commerce and community in an area that usually bustled with activity was surreal. The fear and smoke that permeated the air made my brothers look over their shoulders every few minutes as they helped Mom pick up the debris. The complex across the street was blackened. Mom found out a few days later that the owners had escaped the turmoil and that the 99 cent store owners were also safe. The grocery market owners had also gone unharmed, but the complex was damaged badly and had to be rebuilt.

I made myself busy at home. I vacuumed the living room and tried to fold some laundry. After a while, I turned on the TV and started watching the news. Regular programming had returned to some channels, but others still had live broadcasts. I hoped I could catch a glimpse of the station and perhaps my family. I didn't. Instead I listened to reports of various well-known shops being destroyed – Soon Ja Du's liquor store had been torched to ashes.

At the station, Mom boarded the garage's shattered glass door. Tony and Albert cleaned up the rubble and mess from the break in. As they were cleaning, Mom noticed a Jeep with three troops driving up the street. She went to talk to them.

"Hullo!" she yelled as she flagged them down. "Please stop!"

The soldiers slowed down and got out of their vehicle to talk to her.

"Thirsty?" Mom asked. "Hungry? I give you many sodas and candies."

She pointed to the station about 125 feet from where they stood.

"You can having anything you like. I have waters, peanuts, juice for you."

The soldiers refused at first, but Mom was insistent. They politely thanked her for her offer and tried to tell her that they couldn't take her food, but Mom wouldn't have it. She ran back to the station, grabbed a bunch of stuff, and went back to the soldiers. She put the snacks on the ground in front of them.

"For you," she said as she turned and walked away.

The soldiers picked up the small offering and called out their thanks to her. Many Korean business owners provided food and drinks to the soldiers, grateful for their protection and for just doing their duty. At home, I was beside myself with curiosity. I called the station repeatedly, hoping one of my brothers would answer.

"How's the station?" I asked when Albert finally picked up the phone. "Is it bad?"

"It's a little messed up," he said. "The garage is banged up, but they didn't get into the booth."

"When are you guys coming home?"

"Soon," he said. "I gotta go, we'll see you later."

My brothers, who made sure Mom was all right as she roamed the station, were appalled by the amount of destruction they saw. Broken glass and pieces of looted goods littered the streets and sidewalks. Blackened buildings stood where people used to shop for groceries and purchase money orders. Mom worked to spruce up the station and make it look like it hadn't just gone through days of hellish violence and neglect. She wiped down the pumps, emptied the trash bins, and spoke to a few customers that stopped by for gas. At some point, Eggo showed up.

"Oh, Eggo," Mom said as she patted him on the back. "You okay?"

"*Sí*," he said. "*Bien, bien.*"

"You family?" Mom asked.

"*Mi familia*, okay," he said as he gave her one of his classic loose denture smiles.

Mom was glad to see he was all right.

"It looked like a war zone," Albert said when they finally came home after a few hours. "Soldiers were everywhere, and it was quiet, too quiet."

I couldn't imagine the station being so hushed. It was a hot spot of activity. Whenever I was working in the booth, I couldn't sit down for more than five minutes during a day shift without being bothered by a customer.

By May 4, schools in South Central Los Angeles reopened their doors. Business resumed. Mom was ecstatic with relief. Her business had survived the upheaval. After the riots, people considered Mom lucky. She had escaped the wrath of the civil unrest relatively unscathed. Aside from broken doors and looted items, the station was good. Albert says that people in the neighborhood liked Mom because she'd been in Compton for so long. She was also nice and polite to people. To my amazement, that neighborly camaraderie actually displayed itself in the aftermath of the riots. Albert later told me that folks from the area had helped Mom recover some of the merchandise that had been looted.

"Some guy was rolling a tire toward the garage," Albert said.

He had tagged along with Mom to the station on Monday after school. Mom still wouldn't let me go. Albert told me how people from the neighborhood were actually bringing stuff back. I couldn't believe it. Mom was grateful and thanked them. Cops were also able to recover some looted goods. They drove around in a large truck and asked shop owners to look at some of the merchandise and identify what was theirs and what was not. Everyone was on the honor system. Mom looked at the truck full of stolen goods and found a few items, but her tools, other inventory, and most of her oil were never recovered. Mom's faith in people had been shaken badly during the riots. Mine was completely shattered.

Mom's good neighborhood reputation was very likely what saved her business from burning to a crisp. Perhaps it was because she had always been nice, or maybe it was because of Eggo, or because of some random act of miraculous intervention that the station didn't get destroyed in the violence. Who knows? But Mom was fortunate. Other Korean Americans were not so lucky. Many lost their businesses, their means to survive, to live, and thrive.

The messed-up situations that Korean American business owners were in after the LA Riots resonate to this day. The Korean American community served as a scapegoat for the real problems that caused those riots, the 1965 Watts Riots, and the Baltimore Riots, to name just a few. I was furious. This wasn't right. But what could I do as a twelve-year-old kid? Not a damn thing.

When Rodney King made his famous statement on May 1, "Can we all get along?" I laughed at its futility. To me it seemed every ethnicity was out to help themselves and no one else. So how could we all get along? Officially, the riots ended on May 4, 1992. The weekend after the end of the craziness, Mom felt things were safe again and decided that I could go to work with her. I was ready to help. To work. To fight if I had to. I was ready to go back to the booth.

"Today, be as nice as you can," Mom said as she drove. "Don't cuss at anyone. If you have a problem, get me right away."

"Okay," I said as I started to imagine how I would fend off potential looters and rioters.

I was stunned when we got to the station. The pile of rubble and ash that used to be the stores across the street angered me. The station looked exactly as Albert described it to me. I walked over to the damaged garage bay doors. The metal was disfigured from where the car rammed into it. I thought about what could have happened. What if the rioters had broken in when Mom was still there? What if protestors had pulled Mom out of her car – like they did to Reginald Denny – and beaten her for being Korean?

I put the thoughts aside as I ran to catch up with her as she went inside. I went to the cashier's booth with her. One of the workers was there waiting for us. I surveyed the booth as I greeted him.

"How's everything?" I asked him. "Did you have any problems last night?"

"No," he said as he handed me the inventory book.

I tied my black hair into a tight ponytail and looked up at the cigarettes. I counted them quickly: ten, twenty, thirty, forty. Then I turned to look at the windows. The bulletproof glass had no new marks. No one had shot at it during the riots. We changed shifts, and Mom let me work the first couple of morning hours. The sun rose and the shadows fell in their usual spots. I looked across the street and furrowed my brow. That morning I couldn't go to the donut shop to get coffee. I couldn't go to the market either and buy some fruit. Why? Because rioters had torched the complex. The pillars of burned wood that used to be those businesses stood out like angry, black brushstrokes on a canvas of blue sky. The day wore on, and everyone that came to the window was a suspect to me. Maybe someone would try to rob us? Maybe someone would try to do something. I kept my eyes peeled.

"Hey," a black man said. "Gimme five on eight."

I picked up the man's money and nodded in acknowledgement. *Here we go*, I thought. All day long, people were curt, nice, apathetic, or mean. One customer even muttered a racial slur toward me.

"Chinks still ain't left the hood," he said. "Still haven't learnt your lesson."

As customers came and left, I was glad to see some of the neighborhood regulars that I'd gotten to know over the years still milling about and working in the area. I saw the same parents filling up in the morning on their way to church with their kids. I even saw Eggo stroll by. I waved at him as usual. He rewarded me with a smile.

"*Hola*, Eggo," I said. "*Cómo estás?*"

"*Bien, bien*," he said. "*Y tú?*"

"*Bien*," I said. "You didn't get hurt?"

"No," he said smiling with his dentures slightly slipping off his gums. "*Mi familia está bien.*"

During the riots, Eggo said he stayed in his home, safe from the violence. He tried not to get involved. He never told me if he'd had a hand in helping to keep Mom's business safe, but I like to think that he did. The teacher with the blonde braids also dropped by for her usual menthol cigarettes.

"Glad to see you're okay," she said to me and Mom. "Anything happen to you guys?"

"We're all right," I said. "We just got looted. No one got hurt. That's all we can ask for."

I dropped her cigarettes in the tray. She gave me a friendly nod. That weekend shift was long. I was nice to the customers I knew. I was curt to those I didn't know. I yelled back at the people that yelled at me. Despite Mom's warning, I used racial slurs when someone used one with me. I still hated the people that I didn't know and that weren't kind or civil. In the end, it felt like nothing got better after the riots. Customers came and left and said little about the violence. Everyone just went back to the daily grind; get gas, go to work, go home. There wasn't much change.

Meanwhile, the Justice Department conducted a federal investigation of the Rodney King beating. A retrial of the officers occurred: Officer Laurence Powell and Sergeant Stacey Koon were convicted. Theodore Briseno and Timothy Wind were acquitted. The trial lasted one year and when the verdicts were read in 1993, authorities were prepared for another uprising; nothing happened. I was grateful for that much. I didn't want to ever relive something like that again.[33]

For Korean Americans, *Sa-i-gu* was a wakeup call. When all was said and done, 2,200 Korean businesses had been burned or destroyed during the riots.[34] Of the $1 billion in total damages, Korean Americans suffered $400 million of that cost. The South Korean Foreign Ministry announced it was going to send a delegation to Los Angeles to seek reparation for Korean Americans. During the riots, Koreans were outright targeted. Many businesses that were not run by Koreans put up signs that said "black owned"[35] or "Latino owned." Those people were trying to prevent looters and rioters from mistaking them for Koreans and destroying their shops, according to news reports.

Korean business owners had to do something to help keep their dreams alive. Koreans who tried to defend their businesses were portrayed by the media as gun toting vigilantes. Many were wounded or injured while trying to protect their shops. At some point, the media repeatedly showed Koreans up on the rooftops of their businesses with guns. One report showed a group of Korean Americans banded together at a complex in Koreatown. They were sitting on the rooftop with handguns, shotguns, and other weapons. Some of them were wearing sunglasses and jeans. Others had on vests. I wondered if they were bulletproof.

Today, many of those Korean shop owners suffer from post-traumatic stress syndrome (PTSD). Some don't even want to talk about what happened. During the riots, one Korean American died. Edward Song Lee had gone to a call for help at a Korean business during the riots. He was mistaken for a looter and shot and killed by accident.[36]

Korean Americans silently bore the racism, the tragedies, the misunderstandings, and the blatant neglect by the government before, during, and after the riots. Mom and I sometimes talk about what happened, and we think of the losses, the displaced families and all the Koreans that moved away, went bankrupt, and gave up on the American Dream because of the violence. Many of those stories have gone untold to this day.

The LA Riots were a momentary disruption. Though it changed the community forever in the eyes of historians, it was a moment nonetheless. Today, I admire the human condition for its ability to adapt, forgive, forget, and carry on. Mom did exactly that. She carried on and I kept on working with her.

When I went to school after the riots were over, I was glad to see Natalie was okay. We didn't talk about the riots very much. We just went on as if everything was fine. We continued to trade tapes of the latest pop music. We passed each other in the hall and said hello. It was nice to be in that protected bubble, but outside of my school, the Korean-Black Conflict and racial tension that had preceded the LA Riots continued. In 1994, eighteen Koreans were shot and killed in Los Angeles County alone, according to Criminal Justice Department data. Granted, this is a much better number than the thirty Koreans that were killed in LA County in 1991, one year before the riots, when tensions were the worst. But still...

"Aren't you ever going to sell the station?" I asked Mom one day after school in 1993.

All week long, I'd heard about the continued shootings and killings of Koreans. Mom had told me about a few of them. The continued violence made me dread the idea of going to the station. My hate and anger deepened. No amount of rioting or protesting had changed anything. In fact, the Black Korean Alliance disbanded in December 1992 after the riots because "dialogue" wasn't enough to fix the problems. By 1993 we were still struggling to "get along."

"Mom, this isn't worth our lives," I continued as I sat down at the kitchen table. "Anything would be better than this, let's sell."

She gave me a snack of cut-up apples. Tony and Albert were upstairs in their rooms.

"We could go to Orange County, we could open a restaurant, we could..."

"That's enough," Mom said. "What would I do without the station? Do you think it's so easy for me to go find a job? Do you think it's easy to open another business? No."

I just didn't understand. I didn't get that the station was truly our lifeline. The business provided the roof over my head, the food on my plate, the snack I was eating at that very moment. All we had to do was survive in our environment, to persevere. Mom knew the only way to do that was by working hard. So how could she just sell the station? Even after the riots, she wouldn't budge. She said the riots were part of life.

"You just have to learn to deal with this kind of stuff," she said. "Don't let it bother you."

But how I could I not?

A picture of the garage bay doors at the station. During the riots, the doors were smashed. Mom had them repaired. (Photo from family archives).

89

Chapter 7

YOLO (You Only Live Once)

After the riots, not much changed for me or the area except for the demographics. The city started to get more Latino residents, and the black population slowly started to move away. Sometimes, I'd get into fights with customers, and we'd have our racist slur filled bouts. Mostly, though, I just worked in that crappy little cashier's booth.

"Ain't been burned down, eh?" said a black man a few weeks after the riots.

"Nope," I said as I prepared myself for a fight. "We're still here."

"Your mom's a nice lady," he said as he dropped five bucks into the metal tray. "You lucky."

"What number?" I asked.

"I said, you was lucky."

"And I said what number?"

"You nips never learn," he said. "Number nine."

"Piece of shit," I said as he walked away.

I sat down on my little chair. *Idiot people*, I thought as I shook my head. *He's lucky he didn't get shot by the National Guard. What a jerk.* I stood up and started to count the inventory. We were low on chocolate and flowers. I grabbed a carton of cigarettes, opened the box, and stocked the slats on the wall. I took the empty carton and sat down again, ripping and shredding it until all I had left were tiny pieces. I gathered them all up and tossed them into the trash.

By 1993, I was already traumatized and jaded because of the riots and because of the racism I experienced at the station. But, to make things worse, I soon learned that no matter where I was, I wasn't safe, not even in my own home.

On March 4, 1993 – one month before my thirteenth birthday and the one-year anniversary of the LA Riots, I experienced a whole new kind of fear. On that day, Mom picked us up from school. As usual, she dropped us off at the house. Tony went upstairs to use the phone in Mom's room and watch television. Albert went into the den to watch cartoons. I sauntered into the kitchen and scrounged around the refrigerator for a snack. I also grabbed the two pounds of frozen beef Mom wanted me to defrost for her, put it on a plate, and set it on our brown dining table.

I went into the den and tried to watch some cartoons with Albert. I ate my snack. After about thirty minutes or so, I got sleepy. I went upstairs and plopped down onto my twin mattress, which was pressed into a corner, just the way I liked it. I pulled my orange blanket over my head and fell asleep in my blue school shorts and white t-shirt. About an hour or two later, I woke up. I felt refreshed. It was a Thursday. I still had one more day before I had to go to the station and work. I was happy. As I started to get up, I could hear Tony talking on the phone. I realized I hadn't made the rice yet, so I went downstairs.

"Hello," I said to an Asian guy I hadn't ever seen before as I walked into the kitchen. I assumed he was one of Tony's many friends. He was leaning against the counter, near the sink.

"Hey," he said as he stared at me.

I ignored him after the greetings, like I often did with my brother's friends; they were in high school and I was still in junior high; we had nothing in common. I moved around him as I gathered the rice and the washing bowl. He didn't budge when I placed the bowl into the sink. Annoyed, I looked at him.

"Could you move?" I said.

"Your brother wants to talk to you downstairs," he said in a heavy accent. I think he might have been Chinese. I shrugged my shoulders and put the bowl into the sink. For a moment, I thought about not going to the den. I thought maybe I should get the newspaper, but the thought passed. I went to find Albert.

The den is connected to the first floor of the house by three steps and a large rectangular entryway with no door. The entrance is next to the kitchen and the stairwell leading upstairs. Once down those three steps, the den opens to the left, while to the right there is a closet and a wine bar that's recessed further back so you can't see it until you walk by it. That means there's a little nook between the wine bar and the closet door.

When I started to walk down the three steps into the den, I felt odd. The guy in the kitchen was following me. When I took the last step, another Asian man, wearing a red bandana over his mouth and nose, jumped out from the nook and pointed a gun at my face. I laughed.

"Is this a joke?" I asked with a nervous smile.

"No, it's not," he said. "Get over there and lie down."

I looked to where he motioned with his head. There on the floor, next to our newly purchased black leather couches, was Albert. His hands and feet were bound with duct tape. He was facedown and wasn't moving. When I looked back at the man with the gun, I felt a nudge from behind. The other guy, who had bad acne scars, was standing so close to me I could practically feel his breath on my neck. They walked me to where my brother was, all the while keeping the gun to my head. I lay face down next to Albert. My brother turned his head to look at me. I started to cry.

"Be quiet," the man with the red bandana said.

Scared, confused, worried, I didn't know what else to do, so I cried harder.

"Be quiet!"

He pushed the gun harder to my head. I managed to stifle my sobs, but the tears kept flowing. Albert put his head back down into the carpet. Then the acne-scarred man straddled me from behind as he taped my hands together and shooed his accomplice away.

"Shh," he said calmly. "Don't cry. Shh. This won't hurt. Don't move. Don't cry. Shh."

When he was done binding my hands, he took a piece of that damn silver multi-purpose, pressure-sensitive duct tape and put it on my mouth. He left my feet free. I couldn't stop crying. The two men stayed in the room with us, and I kept thinking, *This can't be it, this can't be it!* So I prayed to God to save us. As the minutes ticked by, the men started to quietly argue. In whispers, they discussed something in a language I couldn't identify. I took a chance and looked up to see what was going on.

The gun was on the floor. The acne-scarred man had a hand to his head as he was shaking it. The other man was gesturing with his hand back and forth between them and Albert. I put my head back down and kept praying. After a while, the two men stopped arguing. The one with the red bandana picked up the gun and went back to the nook by the wine bar. The other one hid in the shadows by the couches.

A few seconds later, I heard Tony coming down the stairs. The steps creaked. I turned my head to see. Tony paused just a few steps from the bottom and looked around. I wanted so badly to scream and yell, to warn him, to tell him to get out, to do something. The man stepped out from behind the nook and bounded up the three steps toward Tony. He pointed the gun at my brother and said something I couldn't hear. Tony put his hands up in the air.

95

They put Tony down on the floor, next to me, facedown as well. His glasses pressed against his face. They taped his hands and feet and put a piece on his mouth, too. The three of us were laid out, execution style. My brothers were quiet. I was a complete mess. The tape on my mouth was moist with tears, and I tried to swallow my sobs. Time was immeasurable. All I know was that when it all started, there was light outside, and by the time all three of us were on the floor, it was dark.

Eventually, my tears eased, and I went quiet, too. After a while the men came toward us and picked up Tony. When Albert looked to see what was going on and saw that they had Tony on his feet, ready to take him somewhere, he tried to yell, but nothing came out, only the muffled sound of his voice.

The guy with the red bandana guided Tony back up the three steps and then up the stairwell. Tony hopped the whole way. I could hear the thud of his feet. The acne-scarred man stayed with me and Albert. He kneeled down next to me and patted me on the head. "This will all be over soon," he said. A couple of minutes later, the guy in the red bandana came back downstairs, grabbed me and stood me up. Albert lifted his head and looked at me. He tried to yell again, but to no avail. He struggled to move toward me, his body writhing on the floor. His older brother protective instincts took over at that moment as he tried to help me. The other guy put a foot on his back and told him to quit moving. I looked at Albert and tried to comfort him. At this point, red bandana guy had let the disguise fall to his neck. I turned to look at him and could see his smooth face. He immediately put the gun to my head and told me to close my eyes. He nudged me forward and guided me with one hand gripping my arm and the other pressing the gun to my head.

"Steps," he said as we walked up the three stairs out of the den. When we got to the stairwell, about four steps up, I couldn't keep my eyes closed any longer. I just remembered being furious, being angry that these two assholes were doing this to us. That in just a few moments, I was probably going to die, and it was going to happen at home. I mean, I had expected something like this to happen at the station. I had always thought that if someone was going to hurt or kill me, it would be some random fucker at the station with a grudge. But nope, there I was, standing on the stairs at my house with some douchebag pressing a damn gun to my head. I wanted to take a good, long look at this asshole who was going to kill me. I opened my eyes and stared at him.

"I said keep your eyes closed!" he yelled loudly as he dug the gun into my scalp. The cold of the steel gave me goosebumps.

"I'm sorry, I'm sorry!" I tried to mumble through the tape. I flinched away from him and closed my eyes.

"Come on, hurry up!" he said.

When we got to the top of those ten agonizing steps, he pushed me forward. I could hear him turning a door knob.

"Open your eyes," he said.

We were in front of the bathroom near my room. Inside, the lights were off. He pushed me in and shoved me with the gun toward the bathtub. He pulled the sliding door aside. I saw Tony, sitting at the end, his knees to his chest.

"Get in," he said. "And keep quiet."

I obeyed. Once I sat down, he slid the water-stained glass door shut, walked out and closed the bathroom door behind him. I started to cry again. Tony was breathing hard. Each breath sounded forced, almost angry. He was trying to get the tape off his mouth. Part of it finally came loose at the corner of his lips.

"It's okay," he whispered. "It's going to be okay, don't panic."

I nodded my head and tried to calm down. But it was hard because all I could think about was Albert with those guys. Who knew what was happening? Then I started to think about Mom and what would happen if she came home to this mess. I panicked all the more. We sat there for a few minutes; there were no more sounds or voices. I was scared for Albert. Why was it so quiet? Where was he? What the hell were they doing with him? *My God,* I thought, *they're going to kill him first!* Then we heard some yelling.

"Tell us!" one of the men said.

"I don't know!" Albert said.

BANG!

Oh my God! They shot him! I thought.

BANG!

No! Please! I thought.

BANG!

Please God! Help us! I prayed.

BANG!

As I sobbed, Tony tried to calm me down.

"No, no," he mumbled through the tape. "No, Carol, they didn't shoot him!"

I shook my head in disbelief. Tears streaming down my face, I imagined Albert dead, like that woman who had been stabbed at the station, blood everywhere. I heard another BANG! I cried more.

"No!" Tony said. "They're kicking a door! They didn't shoot!"

This time I listened to the sound. Tony was right. How many times had I heard gunfire at the station? I knew the difference. I tried to calm myself down and think logically about what was going on. The robbers were kicking the door to Mom's closet. They were trying to find money.

The bangs finally stopped. We heard nothing else for maybe ten or fifteen minutes. Then we heard the front door open and close. My heart felt like it was pounding through my chest. I dared not move. Neither did Tony. So we sat there in the tub for a long time. Probably for twenty minutes or so, I'm not sure. We didn't move. We didn't speak. The only sound was Tony's heavy breathing.

DING DONG!

It was the doorbell. Tony's eyes widened at the sound.

"It's Joe! It's Joe!" Tony yelled through the corner of his mouth. "Go open the door, tell him what happened! Go!"

Mindlessly, I shot up like an arrow. Somehow, I got the shower door open and then the bathroom door. I ran downstairs and used my bound hands to unlock and open the front door. I was face-to-face with Joe, Tony's friend from high school. He stared at me, startled at my disheveled appearance.

"What happened?!" he asked as he tore the tape off my mouth.

"We've just been robbed! Call the cops! My brothers are upstairs!"

Just as I had finished telling Joe everything, I saw headlights coming down the street. I recognized Mom's car. As Joe ran upstairs, I twisted my hands as hard as I could and broke them free of the tape. I ran outside as Mom pulled up the driveway. Sobbing with joy and fear, I pounded on her window. She rolled it down; her eyes were wide with fear.

"What's wrong?" she asked.

"We've been robbed!"

"What?! Where are your brothers?!"

"Inside!"

She got out of her car and ran with me into the house. Albert was sitting on the couch, his fists clenched. Tony was on the phone with the cops. Joe was standing next to him.

"Are you guys okay?!" Mom asked.

"Yes," Albert said evenly. "We're fine."

"The police are coming," Tony said as he hung up.

As we waited for the cops, Joe left. Tony, Albert, and I sat around Mom on our gray living room couch; it was the same gray couch we sat on together just three years prior when she told us Dad died. She hugged us. The cops arrived and searched the area. They walked through the house, took fingerprints, picked up the red bandana the thieves left behind, and asked us a dozen questions.

"You said you had to unlock the door right?" an older white cop asked me.

"Yes."

"Means they probably found a copy of your house key. Change the locks."

That night, we slept at a hotel. It turns out the two men that robbed us were some sort of gang or mafia members who had likely scoped out our house for a while before they hit us. These were professionals, according to the police, who liked to target Asian business owners and their homes because of the potential cash that could be inside. It's just another drawback of being a business owner, especially an Asian one. The rumor is that Asians keep large stashes of cash at home.

The cops said we were lucky. We saw the faces of those men and lived. And the added bonus was that not much was stolen. Mom's wedding ring, watches, and some necklaces they found in her closet was what they got away with. We didn't have any cash in the house except for the twenty bucks Tony had in his wallet; the robbers took that, too.

The robbers gained entry to the house by using a police badge instead of just breaking in. They knocked on the door and flashed it to Albert. He later told us that he had been in the den for a long time, for as long as I had been asleep upstairs, which was for at least two hours. When he told me that, my mind started to race. *Hadn't I heard voices before I fell asleep? Didn't I hear the door open? Why hadn't I been aware?*

I couldn't believe how close we had come to getting killed. When we went to the hotel that night, I tossed and turned. I had a major case of the hiccups. I was pissed that I couldn't fall asleep and the damn hiccups wouldn't go away. I ended up going to the bathroom and drinking several glasses of water. Mom heard. When I came back to the bed, she sat up.

"Are you okay?" she asked.

"Yes."

"Did they hurt you?"

"No," I said.

I think she let out a sigh of relief, but it could have been the air conditioning, I'm not sure. I crawled back to bed and eventually I did fall asleep.

The next day my class was going on a fieldtrip; we were going whale watching. It was still early, and the buses hadn't arrived yet. I went and found my friend Karen. She was a nice white girl I became friends with. She had transferred over from a different private school that year. Karen and I walked around the school's outdoor basketball court as we waited. I told her what happened. She was quiet. She offered little by way of comfort. How could she? We were barely even thirteen.

The buses finally came to pick us up, and I had the fortune of sitting across from a teacher I had nicknamed "Top Nose." Karen was sitting next to me. The principal's wife was in front of us. "Top Nose" was this teacher that I didn't get along with. She used to ridicule me and tell me I smelled or that I was dirty. I called her all sorts of names and made fun of her witch-like nose. Once, I was nearly suspended from school because I told her she was a "mean-old-bitch." Mr. Smith chided me, but let me slide with a warning and the promise that I wouldn't use such foul language again. Fuck if I cared.

"What's the matter with you today?" Top Nose said to me as the bus started to pull out of the parking lot. "You're very quiet, which is unusual for *you.*"

She always said things to me with a snide tone, and I always talked back to her the same way. I tried not to say anything. But she was staring at me with a smug look.

"Fuck you," I said. "Leave me alone."

I turned my head away from her, and I think I started to cry. I can't remember it clearly, though. Whatever the case, I thought I would be in trouble for sure, but for some reason, I don't recall getting busted for cussing. Top Nose didn't do anything. For the rest of the trip, she left me alone. The principal's wife didn't say anything to me either. Maybe she didn't hear what I said. Who knows?

During the drive, my mind raced. I relived the robbery over and over again. The house wasn't safe anymore. I started thinking of ways to fortify entry points at home, much like I did when I was in the cashier's booth. I started to think about how to protect myself. *If I pull the dryer door down in the garage it will keep the side door from opening. If I put bells on the door, we can hear it if someone tries to open it. I should put a bat next to my bed...*

We drove for an hour or so, and I stayed quiet. I tried to sleep but ended up staring at the cars we passed. We ended up at the beach. The boat we boarded to go see whales was beautiful. The luster of its body was accented with blue lines. The other kids were ecstatic at the prospect of the ride we were about to take. Everyone went to the top deck for a better view. I found a smooth white bench and sat down. I didn't care about finding whales. I just wanted to be left alone. I dozed in the warm sunlight. The smell of the sea and the movement of the boat made me feel strange. I tried to think about something other than the waves. Instead, I thought about guns and duct tape. That night, I couldn't sleep a wink.

Months later, the cops showed up at Albert's and my school and told the principal what happened. The cops called me and Albert out of class. (Tony was attending high school at a different location at the time.)

"Sit down, please," said one of the cops.

"Uh, what's this about?" I asked nervously.

"We would like to show you some pictures, young lady, to see if you might be able to recognize the men that robbed you a while back."

"Oh," I said as memories of the incident flashed through my brain.

One of the cops opened a three-ring binder; it held several pages of mug shots. He started to flip through them slowly. I gripped the armrests of the brown chair I was sitting in.

"Do you see anyone you recognize?"

"No," I said as I stared at the faces. I looked hard for the acne-scarred man. "No, I don't."

"Take a real good look," he said.

I stared and stared. Nothing popped out to me. Was I so dumb that I couldn't even remember the faces of the robbers? I stared harder. Still, I saw nothing.

"I'm sorry," I said after a while. "I don't see anyone I recognize."

"Are you sure?"

"Yes."

"Okay," one of the cops said. "Thank you for your time."

When the cops left, I got up to leave.

"Carol," the principal called as I was trying to make my exit. "What happened?"

I turned and looked at him.

"Are you okay?" he asked.

"Great," I said as I stared at him.

"Listen, if you need to talk…"

"Can I go now?"

He nodded his head yes. I walked out as quickly as I could. As I went back to class, I thought about the robbery. One of the other things that shocked me about the incident was that the men that robbed us were Asian. How could Asians do this to other Asians? We all worked so hard and knew each other's pain so well. Hadn't we all just gone through the LA Riots together as a community? That was the day I stopped trusting in the cohesiveness of ethnicity. It dawned on me that I just couldn't trust anyone. Not a single soul. Not a customer, not a cop, not a teacher, or anyone else. I wasn't safe anywhere, not even in my home. I became even more paranoid. Sleeping was difficult. I started to think about what I could use as a weapon to defend myself. Mom wouldn't let me keep knives at the station, but there was at least a bat.

When I went to the station to work the weekend after the robbery, I was a little grateful to be there. Even though it wasn't safe there either, I was still enclosed and protected in that cashier's booth where not even bullets could penetrate. By the way, I hate duct tape, can't use the stuff to this day. And the robbers, they were never caught.

By 1994, I had become cynical, angry, and just downright racist. The robbery made me angrier and added to the mix of crazy I felt. I hated not only my work situation but the fights and the racism that persisted, despite the pretended handholding in the aftermath of the LA Riots. Organizations and associations called for peace between the feuding ethnicities and gangs. But I had no peace. I felt trapped. Nothing was different except for the length of my hair. Violence was still running amuck. Drugs were still a problem. I was still counting cigarettes and candy bars. I was still watching the world pass by me in that booth.

In March 1994, I was working yet another graveyard shift with Mom and Albert. I was people-watching and counting the number of blue cars that came and left. I stood in the booth mindlessly punching the keys. I was tired. Few words were exchanged as I processed the transactions.

A red car pulled up at pump number nine. Disappointed by the color, I watched as a man in a white cowboy hat, a silk shirt, large buckled belt, and tight jeans got out. He put a hand in his pocket. I looked away for a second to see who had just pulled up at another pump. When I looked back toward the man in the hat, he was yelling at someone.

"Get away from me," the man in the hat said. "Asshole!"

Another man was standing in front of the guy in the hat. This new guy was dressed in a blue and black jacket and gloves. He was arguing with the other guy. I stood there in the cashier's booth and just stared at the trouble. Albert was in the back office watching television. I was missing my favorite show, but it was my turn to watch the register. Mom was asleep in our blue van she liked to park in the station's garage every night.

As I watched, the two men got more agitated with each other. The man in the hat gestured with his hand to the other guy and yelled. The guy in the jacket pulled something out. Before my mind could register what I was seeing, the man in the hat lifted his silk shirt and pulled out a gun, too.

The man in the jacket managed to shoot first. The man with the hat fired two or three shots, I can't be sure. The other man squeezed a few more rounds off. The man with the hat and large buckled belt doubled over and then fell backward as he took the bulk of the bullets. His body jerked from the impact of the gunfire. The other man took off running. I screamed and fell to the floor. Doors slammed. People yelled. Cars peeled off. I stayed low and crawled to the office in the back and dialed 911.

"Hello," I said, trying to calm my voice. "There's just been a shooting. Please send someone. I think someone is really hurt."

"Where are you, ma'am?"

I gave the address.

"Did you see what happened?"

"Yes, I saw everything. Could you please hurry and send someone? I think someone is really hurt."

The cops arrived. The man who had been shot managed to crawl across the street to the other gas station. He died over there.

"Good evening, miss," the cop said. "So there was a shooting?"

"Yeah, there was, you missed all the action," I said. "I don't know where the shooter is, but the guy he shot is across the street."

Mom was standing next to me, frazzled by the mayhem. The cop glanced sideways and then back at me.

"Miss, we're going to tape off this area of your business and look at the crime scene. The coroner will be here shortly."

"You going to do something about this?" I asked.

"What can we do? These people kill each other all the time," he said.

Mom and I waited for the cops to clear the scene. Albert came to check on me and asked if I was okay. I shooed him away and told him I would work the next few hours. The adrenaline was still pumping through my veins. Mom stayed in the booth with me.

"Are you hungry?" she asked.

"No," I said.

"Turn on the heater, you look cold."

"I'm fine," I said as I pulled my long, black hair into a ponytail.

"Why don't you go sleep a little?"

"I'm not tired," I said as I started counting coins. We always had a lot of change, and I was constantly wrapping rolls of pennies, quarters, dimes, and nickels. I looked up from my pile of money. Mom's eyes were red from lack of sleep. Her hair was much greyer than it had been since we first started our work life together in 1990.

"Go rest," I said. "Those cops are going to be here for a long time. There's nothing to do, so let me watch the booth for now."

Mom looked at me for a few seconds, and I looked away. I watched as the cops looked for bullet shell casings and went about their investigation.

I could feel Mom's eyes on me like a fierce mama bear staring at her cub. I ignored her.

"Okay," she said. "I'll come back later."

When I went to school the following week, I didn't talk about the shooting to anyone. I didn't mention it to teachers or anyone for that matter. I kept the secret to myself and only spoke about it with my brother. Even then, I didn't talk about it much with him either. I had become numb to the violence, and so I put it out of my mind. Instead, I completed my final year in private Christian school and graduated with my class in June 1994. In the pictures, I look like a fresh-faced, happy Korean girl, getting ready to enter the ranks of the teenaged mania called high school. Most of the kids from my private school went on to other private schools. Only two or three went with me to the public high school my brothers were already attending. Natalie was one of them. I didn't speak to her much in high school except for the occasional acknowledgement in the hall.

When I got to high school, I was thrust into the public school system, where ethnic diversity and larger classes were the norm. I made friends fast and hit it off with a small clique of Asian kids who were known for their studiousness and good manners. I adjusted well in the new environment, where I could cuss freely and no one would threaten to tell on me, and where groups were properly segregated into ethnic cliques: Mexicans hung out with Mexicans; Asians with Asians; Whites with Whites; Blacks with Blacks; and socially awkward leftovers formed their own nerd squads.

There were also gangs and a type of violence that's particular to high school students. All the testosterone and estrogen just breeds a natural kind of crazy in teenagers that didn't involve riots; I liked the public school even more. My own growth hormones were also raging. At the station, those hormones ran amuck, and I would fight with customers more, cussing, yelling, and practically screaming at them as I learned to deal with my emotions, especially anger and hate. However, at school, I was calm and nice. I did my best to fit in. No one yelled at me there. No one told me I was a chink. I had new friends, and I could at least try to be like a well-adjusted kid. That being said, I wasn't living the life of a normal kid in high school.

"Why can't you go out this weekend?" my new friend Cindy asked me.

"I can't," I said. "I have to work."

Work, I thought. *Damn work*. How could I explain to Cindy, or to anyone for that matter, that my life consisted of shift change after shift change and shouting matches with customers I learned to hate just a little more every time I fought with them? How could I explain to her that I didn't sleep well and often times I'd wake up sweating, my heart racing because I'd had another nightmare?

"Can't you get out of it?" Cindy asked.

"No," I said as I sighed.

It was late 1994, and I was discovering a whole new world outside of the small Christian school I had attended practically my whole life. There were things like sleepovers, birthday parties, and going out to the movies. Things I was old enough to do now. There were happy places where I wasn't surrounded by racist assholes and bulletproof glass windows. But those were things I couldn't go to because I had to work. My new friends didn't know anything about my life outside of school. How could I explain it to them? How could I tell them that just a few months before I started high school I was an eye witness to a random murder? Or that Mom knew a pimp? Or that I really, really hated eating certain chocolates simply because I was around them so much?

"Where do you work?" Cindy asked.

"Compton," I said.

We were eating lunch at school.

"Wow," she said.

"I know."

I was happy because I made friends like Cindy at my new school, and I reveled in the fact that I could finally hang out with other Asian kids. But I hated the fact that I couldn't hang out with them more. Whatever the case, I took what I could get because it meant less time at the station. After a few months, my new friends were used to my crazy work life.

"That asshole!" I yelled as I watched a black man take off. "He just stole our squeegee!"

I was mid-stride into my freshman year of high school. The year 1995 saw me turn fifteen years old, still working shifts with mom. My new friends were used to my absence from their birthday events, holiday gatherings, and other teenaged shenanigans that a group of studious kids could get into. As I stood in the booth wondering just how much fun my friends were having that weekend, I turned on the station's speaker system and yelled at the bum who'd just stolen my squeegee.

"Hey, you jerk!" I yelled. "Bring that back!"

The black guy turned and looked my way as he ran across the street toward the other station and gave me the middle finger.

"Asshole!" I yelled.

Seeing that I couldn't do anything to the guy – I couldn't call the police for such a trivial thing – I turned off the speaker and went to the back office.

"Mom, we lost another squeegee," I said. "You know if you keep stocking that stuff these jerks are going to keep stealing."

"Go back to the booth," Mom said.

"That's four this month!"

"I'm tired," Mom said. "Go work."

I went back to the booth and sat down on my chair. I stared at nothing until finally a customer got my attention.

"Yeah," I said.

"Number eight," the black woman said. "Give me fifteen dollars. Give me a chocolate bar, too."

I took her money, punched in the numbers, and dropped the candy in the tray. As she reached for the candy, I shoved the change through and bumped her hand hard.

"Watch what you're doing," she said.

"Whatever," I said.

"Little bitch," the woman said.

"Screw you," I said. "Get the hell out of here."

"I want a refund," she said as she slammed the money and chocolate back

down into the tray.

"No refunds," I said as I turned my back to her.

"Nip, you better give me my money back!"

As we started to cuss and yell at each other, Mom came into the booth.

"What wrong?!" she said in her Korean accent.

"She wants a refund, and it's too late, I already punched in the gas," I said.

Mom turned and looked at the angry woman I had just offended.

"What problem?" she asked the lady.

"She's the problem," the woman said as she pointed her finger at me. "She's being rude!"

"You're the one being a bitch," I said as I glowered at her.

"Stop," Mom said to me in Korean. "Shut up."

"I'm sorry," Mom said to the woman in English. "Please, pump gas."

The woman looked at Mom and then at me.

"You better teach her some manners," she finally said as she walked off toward her car.

"Teach her right if you know what's best for you both."

"Why did you pick a fight?" Mom asked me in Korean. "Stop being stupid!"

"I hate it here!" I said as I hit the metal countertop next to the cash register. "I hate all of them! All they do is cuss at me, tell me I'm a chink, and steal things. I don't want to be here anymore!"

"Don't say those things!" Mom said.

"I don't care what you say. If someone cusses at me I'm going to cuss right back at them."

At that moment, another customer came to the window.

"*Veinte en la siete*," the Mexican man said.

I took his money without saying a word. He walked away.

"See, they don't even speak English! Why do I have to speak Spanish? Huh? I'm so sick of it here."

Maybe I was on a hormonal rampage again or perhaps I was just super tired that day, but whatever the case, I was having a fit. Mom couldn't calm me down. She finally gave up and told me to go to the back office and sleep it off. I happily agreed and slept on that damn gray-tiled floor for hours.

The following Monday, I went to school and saw my friends. I was happy the weekend was over. My friends and I were getting to know each other better. I started to tell them about the funnier things I saw at the station, like people driving off with the pump in their cars, but most of the time I kept the racist, traumatizing stuff to myself.

My one joy in school was English class. I loved to read. I read everything I could. When I was in the fifth grade, attending that private Christian school, I discovered my passion for reading after my favorite teacher, Mrs. Archie, had us watch a movie based on *Anne of Green Gables* by L.M.

Montgomery. Mrs. Archie took us to the screening room – it had that ugly, hard, green school carpet that smelled from years of use – we all sat down in front of a large television. I crossed my legs and reveled in the moment. I was ready to take a nap on a floor that wasn't made of gray tile. I could sleep and not worry about Mom coming to wake me up to take over a shift for her. I could rest in peace! But the opening scene hooked me and I couldn't keep my eyes off the screen.

Anne was walking through the woods, a book in one hand, a lunch basket in the other. She was reading. She was daydreaming. She was on her way to give lunch to her foster father. As she neared his place of work – a wood mill – she saw him fighting with someone and then he collapsed. The movie continued, and I was enthralled by Anne's story and her hard life. Anne was just a kid, like me, living a messed-up childhood. She was an outcast, an orphan who had to work hard just to keep her place in a foster family that didn't want her. Her only escape from reality was through books. I watched the movie, engrossed in every little detail. I was enraptured. As Anne went through the trials and tribulations of youth, I connected with her and found myself wondering if I couldn't also escape through reading. When the movie was over, I walked up to Mrs. Archie.

"Is the movie based on a book?" I asked.

"Yes," she said. "We have them all in the library."

All! I thought. *That means there's more to the story!*

At lunch, I went to the library. I asked the librarian where I could find *Anne of Green Gables*. She was an older lady; her hair was that dyed reddish brown that makes you think of an old leather jacket. She smiled and walked with me to get it. The library's narrow aisles, with its rows and rows of books, reminded me of the tiny cashier's booth, only friendlier. The library smelled sweet, not like the station where gasoline and car exhaust fumes saturated the air and wrinkled my nose. I took the first book in the series with me to the station. I ate up every word. I lived in Anne's world, in a place where there were no such things as stray bullets or twenty-four hour shifts. I was so engrossed in the words that I didn't notice Mom walk into the booth.

"Carol," Mom said. "Carol!"

I was focused on a scene in the book; Anne had just found out she was going to be adopted by Marilla and Mathew Cuthbert. She wouldn't have to do backbreaking work anymore; cooking, cleaning, and taking care of her foster parents' family. She was going to be free!

"What are you doing?" Mom asked. "Why didn't you stock the cigarettes?"

"It's not busy," I said as I dog-eared the page I was on.

"Stop reading. Go get the cigarettes."

"I'll do it in a few," I said.

"Do it now," she said. "Hurry up."

I dropped the book onto the countertop and looked at her. But what could I do? In that little booth, I read countless books. I lived in a world where gas stations had yet to be invented. I read books on the life of Mozart and Beethoven. I read fun books and odd books. In high school, I wanted to keep finding books like *Anne of Green Gables*. I even spent the better part of my first few weeks as a freshman at the library volunteering just so that I could learn how to catalog books and peruse the school's collection. I found things like the story of Geronimo. I even came across the *Little Women* series by Louisa May Alcott. My desire to read and learn more about literature drove me to enroll in English Honors, which was headed by a veteran teacher: Mrs. Meads. She was a spry woman who looked to be in her mid-fifties. Her permed hair was short and grey. Her glasses were a little too big for her wizened face. She spoke with her hands, and she fascinated me with her enthusiasm.

She saw my passion for reading, for writing, and for books. She encouraged me and recommended things for me to read, things like *Medea* and *Oedipus*. She seemed to genuinely care, and I often hung out in her classroom during lunchtime with my friends. I talked with her about school and the things I read. She always listened to me and was kind. She earned my trust because she treated me with respect. She was the first teacher I told about my life as a cashier. A few months into my freshman year, I ended up telling her about the shooting.

"You're always so tired," Mrs. Meads said after I finished telling her about it. My friends were chattering with each other and not listening to my conversation with her.

"I know," I said. "Sometimes I have trouble sleeping."

Mrs. Meads gave me a look, a look I hadn't seen since Mr. Smith recommended counseling for me and Albert all those years ago.

"I gotta go," I said before she could say anything else.

I rejoined my friends and tried my best to ignore Mrs. Meads' concerned look. I tried not to talk to her again. After about a week, I felt sure she'd forgotten what I told her and moved on. After all, she must have heard a thousand stories like that from other students over the years. When it was time for English class, I trotted happily into the room. Today, we were going to go over a reading assignment. Class hadn't officially started yet, so I sat down at my desk and rummaged through my back pack.

"Carol," Mrs. Meads called out to me. "Can you come here please?"

I got up and went to her desk. *Had I messed up the homework?* I wondered.

"Today, I'd like you to go to the main office," Mrs. Meads said. Her blue eyes bore into me. "From now on, every Thursday I'd like you to go the main office instead of here."

"Why? I'm going to miss class."

"Don't worry. I'll give you the notes."

She sent me on my way. *What the heck was going on? Was I being punished?* I shrugged my shoulders and walked to the office.

"Hi, Mrs. Meads told me to come here for this period," I told the office assistant.

"Oh yes," the woman said. "Please go into that room."

I tried to see into where the lady pointed at, but the blinds were closed. I walked over and opened the door.

"Good, you're here," a pretty-looking woman said to me. "Take a seat."

I wasn't the only student in the room. I recognized one other girl, a Mexican kid who was also in Mrs. Meads' class but in a different period. There was a black boy and a black girl as well. I didn't know them.

"Uh, what's this about?" I asked.

"Just have a seat," the lady said. "I'll explain in a minute."

I sat down in one of those uncomfortable plastic school chairs with the round metal disks at the bottom of the legs. I hated those chairs; they felt too small.

"Welcome, everyone," the woman said. "You're here today because one of your teachers recommended you for this very special class."

What the hell is this? I started to get nervous.

"We're here today to talk about things," she continued. "To learn about each other. To help each other."

Oh hell no! I thought.

"I want to get to know you and understand you," she said. "So let's start by giving each other our names. I'm Linda."

Dammit, dammit, dammit. This is one of those "I care about you" bullshit counseling things, I thought as the other kids gave their names.

"I'm Carol," I said when it was my turn. "Look, I think there's been a mistake. I don't need to be here. Can I go?"

"It's okay, don't feel like this is a bad thing," Linda said. "Here you're safe. You can talk about whatever you want."

"With everyone else listening?" I asked. "Really?"

In Korean culture, you don't talk about your personal life to others, much less anything traumatizing. It's hard enough that the Korean American community is just a small slice of the American pie, add to it our silent suffering, and it just makes things more difficult. That's why after the LA Riots, people like Mom and other Korean Americans didn't say much and still carry the anger, bitterness, sadness, and whatnot to this day.

"Yes, Carol, we're all here to support each other," Linda said as she pulled out blank sheets of white paper. "Now, let's start off with an exercise."

She passed sheets of paper around. The other students seemed cool with what was going on. Linda took out some colored pencils and markers, and put them in the center of the long table we were all sitting at.

"Now, I'd like for you all to draw yourselves in a setting, any setting. Take your time and really enjoy this," she said with a big, annoying smile. "Imagine yourselves in a happy place, and draw whatever comes to your mind."

I rolled my eyes. *Seriously. This is not happening!* I thought as I rubbed the back of my neck.

"Carol, what color would you like to start off with?" she asked.

I saw no way out of this. What could I do? I decided to comply.

"I'll take the black marker," I said.

For twenty minutes, we drew. Finally, Linda told us to put our colors down. It was time to "share." We went around the table. The room was painted white, our wood-laminated table looked awkward in the setting. I looked around and wondered if the principal was nearby.

"Carol, would you like to share what you drew?" Linda asked.

I flipped over my sheet like it was a work of art. I sat up straight and adjusted my navy-blue shirt.

"This is me, swinging on a vine, off a cliff, with the sun shining. I'm smiling."

The woman looked at me for a few seconds. Was I screwing around? Of course. Did she get it? Of course not.

"Wow, well, I see that you drew a nice, big sun," she said. "But your body is just a stick figure. You have no definition to it while the cliff and the vine are clear."

"I can't draw," I said.

"That's okay, Carol. But I'd like you to think about how you see yourself next time and try drawing yourself with more substance."

"Sure," I said. "Whatever you want."

She nodded her head in what felt like self-approval.

"All right, well, we're out of time, see you guys next week," she said with a smile. I wanted to slap the joy out of her face so badly. Instead, I walked out of there like a bat out of hell. I went straight to Mrs. Meads' room.

"Hello, Carol," she said. "How was your special class?"

"Mrs. Meads, why did you put me in there?"

She furrowed her brow as she considered my question.

"You need it," she said.

"No, I don't. It's a waste of time. I don't want to go back."

"You have to."

"No. I'll not."

"Carol, if you don't go, then I'll be very strict with you and your grade. I know how much you want to get into English Honors II."

"I don't care. Be as strict as you want, but I'm not going back there. It was retarded. The whole thing was ridiculous, and it's not going to help me. No one can, least of all that smug lady."

I stared at Mrs. Meads. The anger I felt when I was working at the station started to surface right then and there in her classroom. Students were starting to walk in for the next period. I didn't give two shits. I mean, it wasn't like I was fighting with anyone at school. I was calm. I did my best

113

to not let work life taint my school life. I never got in trouble for being bad in high school, so why was Mrs. Meads doing this to me?

"Well?" I asked.

"Fine, but this means you have to get a solid A in my class. Otherwise I won't sign you into English Honors II next year."

"Don't worry, I'll get that A," I said.

"Okay, it's a deal then, only an A," Mrs. Meads said.

"Great," I said as I turned to leave.

Throughout my freshman year, I tried to study as much as I could. I took Bio Honors with Mr. Hagino, English Honors, and math. I struggled. I never had enough time to study, but I made sure to work hard on my English homework. I was going to get that A no matter what. I worked my tail off in Mrs. Meads' class and succeeded. While I excelled in English, History and the other arts classes, I sucked terribly at science and math. (So much for Asian stereotypes). I had the hardest time in Mr. Hagino's biology class. In his class I was often absentminded and didn't pay attention because I had no clue what he was talking about; I hadn't done the reading.

"Carol!" Mr. Hagino yelled one day during class. "What are you staring at?!"

He had stopped lecturing mid-sentence when he noticed I had been staring off into space.

"Um," I stammered. "The fish tank."

"Get out," he said. "Stand outside. If you're not going to learn, there's no use in you sitting in my classroom."

My friends looked my way. Their eyes were wide as I stood up and glowered at Mr. Hagino.

"I hate you," I said as I started to walk out the door. I tried to slam it shut, but it had one of those devices that made the door close slowly. As I stepped outside, I heard Mr. Hagino laughing at my feeble attempt at defiance. I was furious. How many times had he kicked me out of class that year? All for what? Just because I wasn't paying attention? My mind drifted to the station as I stood there; the coolness of the day didn't help my disposition. I stared at the grass fields where other students were having PE class. I sank down to the ground and rested my back against the brick wall and put my head on my knees. At least I had some peace and quiet, a moment's rest away from school and from the cashier's booth.

By June of 1995, I had finished freshman year with a grudge against Mr. Hagino and a promise to him that I would take his Advanced Placement (A.P.) Bio course my junior year, like my brothers before me, and annoy him in that class as well. He laughed at me and said he'd let me in just so that he could have the pleasure of kicking me out of that class as well, and to remember that I'd have to take summer school with him before the start of my junior year.

"Until then, good riddance," I said to him.

The summer of 1995, right before the start of my sophomore year, Mom and I worked. One of the employees quit, and we picked up the Monday through Friday, 2 PM – 10 PM shift. We still worked the weekends from 6 AM Saturday morning to Sunday night at 10 PM. The issues and racism I experienced over the weekends were the same on the weekdays. The added workload made me hate the station and the people more than ever. I was furious all the time. I couldn't hang out with my new friends. I couldn't do much of anything but work and work some more. I'd stare at the gold-rimmed clock in the cashier's booth, the same one that had been there since God knows when, probably since Dad bought the place in 1974. I'd stare out the bulletproof windows and pretend to ignore the things I saw: a guy beating up another man; a woman getting hit by either her pimp or her boyfriend; another accident where someone slammed into another vehicle with a car full of kids, and so on and on. The daily routine of shift change after shift change, counting inventory, sorting cash, and going home, made me crazy. I fought with my brothers more and more. I'd yell at them for not coming to help. We'd hit each other, throw stuff, and cuss up a storm. Albert and I would get into some wicked fights. Once he broke one of those flimsy plastic flashlights on my arm – I had the sense to block the blow. I retaliated by throwing my desk chair at him. He pushed me down and walked away. I ran after him. Mom got between us and broke up the fight.

When sophomore year (September 1995 - June 1996) started, I was grateful. No more weekday shifts. Mom hired a temporary worker. That year I tried to be a normal high schooler. So, to help relieve my stress and in an effort to have fun, I volunteered to be the class mascot. The advisor decided that it would be fun to keep my identity a secret. I was a white tiger. One of the students made a mask out of papier-mâché, and I wore an all-white outfit to match. During school rallies, I would dress up and run

115

out in front of my class' section of the bleachers and dance around. I loved every second of it. I could be happy and sheltered behind the white tiger's mask. No one could see the shape of my eyes or call me a racist name. No one could pick a fight.

Mom's reaction to my newfound love of white tigers: "Don't waste your time. Study." Tony and Albert just laughed. For one glorious school year, I paraded around as the mascot. When the yearbook was released and my identity was revealed, the kids that didn't know it was me were shocked. I wasn't the type to do something like that. I was the innocent-looking Korean girl who should fit those stereotypes about docile Asian females. My friends, however, knew me better than that and understood that I needed the outlet. They knew my weekend life was a far cry from typical teenage activities. My new friends and I were getting closer. We could talk. I'd tell them a little more about my other life as a cashier, and they'd listen with genuine concern. But still, I held back some of the scarier, crazy things I'd seen.

By the summer of 1996, right before the start of my junior year in high school, I was as mean as ever to customers. I was sixteen and hitting the height of teenaged insanity. I got into so many fights at the station that I couldn't even keep count. Once, I even kicked one of the station's doors after a particularly bad argument. The door didn't shatter, but it did crack. I never told Mom that it was me who broke it; I blamed it on a customer.

"Mom, other kids don't work like I do," I told her one day while we were in the kitchen cooking dinner. "I really hate it."

"Get the garlic," she said to me in Korean.

"I'm being serious," I countered. "What would you do if I joined a gang? Ran off?"

"Put the soybean paste in the soup," she said as she cut up some onions.

"Don't you see how mad I'm getting? How angry I am?"

She put her knife down and turned to look at me.

"When I was your age, I was already working on the farm from dawn till dusk. My fingers bled. My back ached. If I had let that bother me and make me angry like you, I would not be standing here making this soup for you and your brothers."

"Well, I'm sick of the booth, and I'm not working this summer," I said.

"Stop complaining and come here and learn how to make this soup properly," she said. "Cut up the green onions."

When summer started in 1996, I didn't have to work those weekday shifts after all. I convinced Mom that if I didn't take the A.P. Bio summer school prep course with that jerk Mr. Hagino, I'd fail his class. She reluctantly agreed and made sure the temporary worker she hired the summer before stayed on. As much as I hated Mr. Hagino, I'd still rather be yelled at and tortured by him than spend another second in that damn booth. He was at least yelling at me for a good cause, my education.

Chapter 8

Waiting to Exhale

When I started summer school I was ready to prove to Mr. Hagino that I wasn't just a dumb kid who couldn't remember the difference between mitosis and meiosis. When I started that A.P. Biology class, it was killer, and I wanted to prove to the teacher that I could do well, even though science was not my thing. So, I studied. Mom had always told me that I had to do well in school no matter what. That's why I was surprised when in late July, the day of a big biology test, Mom tried to convince me not to go to school. I was shocked. We argued all through the morning. What she said was the antithesis of what she had always told me about school: never miss a day. For Koreans and Asian Americans in general, education is the path to success and the path to not having to work jobs that make your fingers bleed or your back ache. Good grades were essential, and that meant always going to school, studying hard, and being diligent. I insisted on going to class. Mom wouldn't budge, so I walked to the car, got inside, and waited for her.

"Just stay home today," Mom said again as she got in and sat down in the driver's seat. "Stay home."

"No. I have a big test today, Mr. Hagino won't let me make it up if I miss," I said. "I've been studying for this thing for two weeks! I have to go. Come on, I'm going to be late."

"No, don't go."

"Why?"

She looked at the steering wheel for a moment, contemplating what she was about to say. She closed her eyes. I could see her take a deep breath.

"Last night, I had a dream," she finally said as she gripped the wheel with both her hands. "Your father came to me and told me to keep you in the house today. Something bad will happen to you if I don't keep you home."

I laughed.

"Come on, Mom, you know I don't believe in that kind of stuff. Besides, I'm going straight to school and then I'll come straight home. Nothing can happen to me. I promise I won't go anywhere. Now can we go? I have to get to class."

"Just be careful, okay?"

"I will."

I took that test on mitosis. I felt pretty good about it. I lingered a bit after class and chatted with some friends. I tried to call home and see if Tony or Albert could come pick me up. No one answered, so I asked my friend for a ride.

"Sure, I'm giving a couple of other people rides, too. Want to wait with me in the parking lot?" Cameron said.

I told him I didn't mind at all and thanked him for offering me a lift. We walked over to his red car; one of his friends was already there. We just needed to wait for two other people, and we would be on our way. Cameron and his friend got into the car. I sat on the trunk while we waited. A couple of minutes later, I saw them walking toward us. I recognized them and waved. As I was getting ready to go and greet them, the car started to move. I hadn't noticed that Cameron had started the engine. I didn't know what to do so I held onto the car. I didn't think to get off.

He backed out quickly and drove fast down one side of the parking lot. I held on as tightly as I could to the edge of the trunk which offered little by way of a grip. He made a turn. We headed down a small straightaway. He sped up as he made another turn to go back to his original parking spot. It was a hot day. As he made that turn, I remember thinking I was thirsty. I thought about the movie I had rented the other night: *Waiting to Exhale*. I looked toward the school and saw a student using one of the pay phones. He yelled at me, "What are you doing? You better get off that car!" That's the last thing I remember.

From what people tell me, Cameron had made the turn so fast that I flew off the car and hit the pavement head first, smacking my elbow against the ground in the process. Cameron parked his car and ran out with his passenger to see if I was okay. The other passengers rushed over as well. They gathered around me as I tried to get up.

"I've got to go home," I said. "My mom's going to be so mad."

They told me to lie down and not move. As they watched over me, some other friends came to see what the commotion was about. Someone else had gone to get help. As I lay there, people said that I was complaining about my arm. They thought I had broken it. A parent of one of the students came over and tried to help calm the situation. She told people not to move me and asked if someone had called 911. They nodded. As the minutes passed, friends later told me that I started throwing up. Cameron ran and got a towel from his car and tried to keep me from ruining my clothes.

After a few more minutes, they said my eyes rolled into the back of my head, and I passed out. I was still vomiting. It took the ambulance fifteen minutes to find the parking lot. When they got there, they cut off my favorite white polo shirt and my black jeans with scissors so they could stabilize me. They put me on a gurney and shoved me into the ambulance. When my mom got the call at the gas station that I had been in an accident, she wasn't surprised, she told me later.

"Your daughter broke her arm, and she's being taken to a local hospital," a school official told her over the phone.

Mom worried but was glad it wasn't too serious. She called my brothers and told them what happened. Tony was the first one to get to the hospital near the school. When he arrived, they told him that I had been transported to a hospital in Long Beach. Tony walked into the emergency room and asked for me. A doctor met my oldest brother and explained the situation.

"She has an acute subdural hematoma," the doctor said. "Her arm is fine, just a little scratched."

"What does that mean?" Tony asked.

"Her head injury is severe," the doctor said. "Blood is filling in the area around and possibly inside her brain. We need to evacuate the blood and relieve the pressure. She may have some brain damage. Is your mom here yet? We need her to sign some paperwork."

"She's on her way," Tony said. He was stunned by the news. I hadn't broken my arm; I had broken my head!

Meanwhile, Mom went to the wrong hospital, the one near the school. They tracked me down and told Mom to go to Long Beach. She swung by the house and picked up Albert. When they got there, Tony was waiting.

"Where's Carol?" Mom asked him in Korean. "How's her arm?"

Tony tried to keep his cool and not freak her out with the bad news.

"Mom, Carol didn't break her arm; she's hurt worse than that," he said slowly. "Mom, you've got to go sign some papers."

"What do you mean?" Mom said nervously. "Where's Carol?"

Tony filled her in.

"Carol hit her head," he said. "She's unconscious. The doctors need to operate. You have to sign these papers."

Mom signed the documents. Tony saw her worried expression. She hadn't looked like that since the home invasion robbery, he recalled later. For almost three hours, they waited for an update from the doctors. Someone finally came and talked to them about my condition. The doctors performed a craniotomy and took out a large piece of my skull. The bleeding was so bad the doctors thought I might have a brain hemorrhage as well as the acute subdural hematoma. That posed a problem because if there was one, they weren't sure they could fix it.

"Mrs. Park, if we find too much blood and damage in your daughter's brain, can we let her go on the table?" one of the doctors asked.

Mom was so shaken she couldn't make the decision. She discussed it with my brothers. They talked about what I would have wanted.

"Carol wouldn't want to be alive if she was a vegetable," Tony said to Mom.

"She wouldn't want to live if she wasn't the same person anymore because of this," Albert said. "If it's so bad that she can't even breathe or think anymore, she'd want to be let go."

Mom listened to what my brothers said. She thought about me and what I would have wanted, but still, she couldn't make the decision. Crying, she told Tony and Albert to decide. When the doctors came back, Tony spoke to them on Mom's behalf.

"If there's too much damage, if it's too massive, you have permission to let Carol go," he said to the doctor.

Later, when Tony told me what happened, I was stunned, yet I was grateful because it would have been the right decision. I didn't want to ever be a burden to my family. Time ticked by, and a few of my friends came to the hospital and waited with my family: Cindy, Annie, Angella, a few others, and Cameron. The operation took a while. When the doctors finished, they updated Mom again.

"Mrs. Park, during the surgery we found more blood than expected," the doctor said.

Blood had pooled on my left temporal lobe, causing pressure on my brain to build. The doctors cut out a triangular piece of my skull and evacuated the blood. However, during the operation. they noticed more blood had collected near my ear. They removed a total of two ounces of blood. Once they were sure they had gotten all of it, they put the piece of skull back and closed the incision with twenty-five staples.

"Is she going to be okay?" Mom asked.

"She's going to have a long recovery," the doctor said. "There was a lot of blood. She could have brain damage. She may not be able to speak or understand what you're saying. There might even be some vision loss. We have to wait and see."

I was taken to intensive care after the surgery. For two days, I was unconscious. I only remember a couple of things from the accident before waking up in the hospital. One was an oxygen mask coming toward my face. The second was something that changed my outlook on life and my circumstances. Something that would make me see beyond the cashier's booth, the racism, and the whole kit and caboodle of crazy I had lived through until that moment of my sixteenth year of life.

Somehow, while I was unconscious, I knew something was wrong and that I was fighting for my life. I was begging for it. I was desperate. *Please,* I pleaded to God. *Not like this. Not now. Not after everything that has happened with Dad, the station, the riots, the robbery, everything! Please give me a chance! Give me a chance to live! I'm too young! I'm only sixteen! Please!*

The next thing I remember from the accident is waking up in the hospital. I had tubes in practically every orifice of my body. My head hurt like a truck had slammed into it. If the mechanic bay doors at the station had feelings, perhaps this is what they felt like after the car rammed into them during the LA Riots. I felt nauseous. I still had no clue what had happened. I heard Tony's voice.

"Carol," he said. "Me and Mom are right here. You were in an accident. You hurt your head. But you're going to be okay. Rest."

I looked over at him. Mom was standing next to my bed with him. I tried to talk, but I couldn't. I felt so dizzy. I was confused. All I knew was that my head hurt like someone had hit it with a sledgehammer. Mom held my hand. As I looked at them, I suddenly picked up the scent of macaroni and cheese. I passed out.

A few hours later I woke up again. This time it was because a nurse was inserting a tube in my mouth. Scared, I grabbed the tube as it was being shoved down my throat. In the process, I ripped out the IV in my arm. As I yanked the tube away from the nurse I screamed, "What are you doing?!" The tube felt slick in my hand. I threw it to the side. I tried to gain my bearings but my head ached.

"Calm down," the nurse said as she restrained me. "We're trying to help you! You've been throwing up in your sleep, and we're trying to evacuate your stomach to help you stop."

I didn't understand what they were talking about. I tried to push the nurse away. At that moment, other nurses had rushed into the room and helped restrain me. I struggled. After a few moments, I passed out again. After that, the doctors kept coming to check on me. From that incident, it was clear that I could move, speak, and comprehend what I was being told. Every few hours my main neurosurgeon Dr. Raymond or a nurse would wake me up.

"Carol," the doctor said to me as I awoke. "Can you move your toes for me?"

I opened my eyes. Groggy, I stared at him trying to understand what he asked.

"Medicine," I said. "Please. My head."

I couldn't take the pain.

"Can you wiggle your toes?" he asked again.

I tried to move my feet, hoping that if I complied he would give me something for the pain. My toes felt stiff. I held my breath and tried again. They moved.

"Good," Dr. Raymond said. "Now can you squeeze my hand for me?"

He put his hand in mine and I tried to squeeze, but it was hard. I closed my eyes tight and tried again.

"Good," he said. "Good."

He reached into his coat pocket and pulled out a little flashlight. He clicked it on and shined it into my eyes.

"Follow the light for me," he said.

I tracked it and blinked at the brightness.

"Excellent," he said. "Very good. Now rest."

Before I could ask for more medicine, I passed out again. By the fourth day I was moved to regular care. I was conscious and talking. Mom and Tony visited as often as they could. Friends dropped by intermittently. A couple of distant cousins on my mom's side visited as well. My pastor and his family also came by. I felt loved. I felt safe. As I lay in the hospital bed with twenty-five staples in my head, I worried about Mom. I worried about the business. I wasn't there to help. *Who was working the graveyard shifts?* I wondered.

"Carol," Mom said softly one night when she came to visit. "Are you awake?"

"Yes. Albert? Tony?" I mumbled through the pain.

"We're here," they said.

Mom sat down beside my bed, and my brothers took seats next to her. They started to chat, and Mom stroked my forehead carefully. My head throbbed. I was happy for the painkillers even though they didn't dull the ache completely. Tony and Albert were fiddling with a bag they brought with them. I could smell fried chicken. Oh, how I salivated. But I wasn't allowed to eat yet. Mom and I shared a love for fried chicken. When she and Dad dropped by one of the other stations in Long Beach, Mom would go next door to one of those name brand places to get a single chicken leg and eat it. To this day she loves fried chicken; even though she can't eat it as often as she used to, she'll still sneak a bite here and there. I looked over at Mom.

"Who's working?" I asked.

"Don't worry!" Mom said. "Why are you worrying about that?! Rest!"

Albert didn't visit me as much as Mom and Tony did, but that's because he was the one who covered my shifts on the weekend and helped Mom while I was in the hospital. He came twice to see me. The first time was with Mom and Tony. The second time he came, he was sitting in a chair next to my bed. Mom had stepped out for coffee. I turned to look at him and said, "I'm really glad to see you, Albert." I reached out to pat his hand. Instead of reciprocating this moment of sibling love, he decided to flip me off with both hands and gave me a cheesy, stupid smile.

"What are you doing in here?" he asked.

I laughed and passed out again. I was in the hospital for a total of seven days. The doctors said my recovery was unique in that I didn't have any severe problems; I didn't suffer any brain damage and my body nearly recovered completely. At the time, Dr. Raymond called me his "miracle" patient. I should have had some sort of problem from the injury. Instead all I have is a long scar on the left side of my head, some headaches, and a lack of smell. (Though that seems to come and go). Those symptoms are nothing compared to what could have happened.

While I was in the hospital, I thought about my life, my family, and all the things that had happened after my dad died. It had been a rough six years since 1990. I had become an adult. I realized being bitter and angry only made my life harder than it already was. Once again, I had survived, but this time was different. This time I felt the joy of living through something. Rather than learning to be paranoid and feeling sadness and pessimism – like I did with the robbery, shooting, and other things I saw – I decided to make peace with my life. The twenty-five staples in my head reminded me that it could have all ended that day, so what was I holding on to this anger for? I was squandering my youth and vitality on shit like racism and hatred. Sure, working was hard, but at least I was alive and healthy enough to do it. Isn't that what Mom had been trying to tell me all these years?

The hours I spent laying in that hospital bed offered me a reprieve, but the constant beeping of my heart monitor and the sounds of other sick and injured children gave me a dose of somber reality. All this time I harbored so much hate for the station, and the people that lived in that area. For what? All this time I didn't understand my own Korean American identity. I only knew that people saw my slanted eyes and thought I was another oriental come to take the riches of the American Dream. Korean Americans had no voice, no presence in mainstream American society. After the LA Riots, the birth or rebirth – depending on who you ask – of Korean American identity occurred. Yet, I still knew little about my heritage except for what Mom tried to teach me. I had much to think about.

When Cameron came to visit me, I wasn't mad at him. He was very apologetic and tried to be cheerful.

"It's okay," I said. "It was an accident. I'm okay. We're okay."

By the fifth day of my stay at the hospital, I could get up and take short walks. One of the nurses, Lisa, came every few hours to walk with me. I never forgot her kindness.

"I can't wait to go home!" I told her as we walked through the corridors of the hospital's children's ward.

"What are you looking forward to?" she asked.

"Eating!" I said as I admired the colorful murals of sea animals on the wall.

I hadn't had a bite of food since the morning of the accident. I craved fried chicken, ice cream, rice, and all sorts of Korean foods. Lisa laughed.

"Just a few more days and you might be able to," she said.

I had been recovering quickly. The pain was subsiding, and the medication was working. The fact that I was up and about was a miracle in and of itself. Mom checked on me every day. It was the first time since I started working at the station that I felt her love. For the last six years, all she and I did was work, fight occasionally over shift changes and my mistakes, and then work some more. The accident put things in perspective for both of us.

Mom isn't the type of woman to express her feelings with words. In my whole life, she's told me she loves me only a few times. By that I mean if you were to count on one hand how many times she's uttered those three words to me, you'd be nowhere near the thumb. One of those times she said she loved me, or at least I think she did, was when I was in the hospital. I'm not sure which day it was, but it must have been when I was still in ICU. Mom was next to my bed. She was holding my hand and saying something to me in Korean.

"*Sarang hae*," she said.

Was I dreaming? Did Mom just tell me she loved me? Where the heck was I? I opened my eyes and looked at her.

She stared back at me. "You're awake!"

Years later, and I mean like twenty years later, I confronted her about this supposed moment. We were sitting in the car waiting for my brother; he had gone into the store to get something. He was taking his sweet time, so I decided to take this opportunity and talk to her.

"Do you remember when I got into that accident?" I asked.

She didn't acknowledge my question, so I continued.

"One of those nights you came to the hospital. You were by yourself. You were holding my hand and I think you said 'I love you' to me, but all these years I was never sure. So, did you?"

An awkward silence followed my inquiry.

"The doctor said you may not wake up and that I should talk to you," she said after what felt like ages. "So I did. I came that night without your brothers. You were unconscious still."

"So you're telling me you said you loved me?"

"Talking to you worked, didn't it? You opened your eyes."

I laughed at Mom's refusal to own up to the fact that she said she loved me. Once again, her strong Korean mother's attitude prevailed. At least this time, she was smiling.

The day I left the hospital, I still had the staples in my head, I was still suffering from vertigo every time I got up from bed, but everything else was fine. My hair was growing back in the area where it was shaved. I wasn't as tired anymore. I was looking forward to finally going home. Mom came to the hospital that morning to pick me up.

"Are you all right?" she asked.

"Yes," I said.

"Are you sure she's okay to go?" she asked Dr. Raymond who had come to see me off.

"Mrs. Park, don't worry, she's fine," he said.

As they talked, someone brought breakfast. I no longer had an IV in my arm. I wanted to try eating. Mom saw me go for the food and came to help me. She cut a piece of French toast.

"Try to eat as much as you can," she said to me as she fed me a bite.

I put the bread in my mouth and started to chew. I savored the sweet, buttery taste. I swallowed, but halfway through I gagged and started to throw up. Mom grabbed a towel for me.

"What happen?" she asked Dr. Raymond.

"It seems she hasn't eaten in so long, her body isn't used to the food so she gagged," he said. "Don't worry, though, she just needs to take it easy and eat slowly."

I stopped throwing up after a few dry heaves; there was nothing in my stomach. Mom wiped my sweaty face for me and then helped me into a wheelchair. Dr. Raymond patted my hand and told me he'd see me in a week for my follow-up. I smiled and said thank you. The ride home was quiet and pleasant. Mom said very little except things like, "Be careful, don't hit your head against the window." "Am I driving too fast?" When we got to the house, my brothers welcomed me. I looked at the gray couches, the piano in the corner, and the tiles on the floor. I was happy. I took a good whiff of home as I inhaled deeply; the smell of kimchee and a fresh pot of cooking rice comforted my aching head.

Mom helped me into the kitchen and started pulling things out of the fridge. She set a jar of spaghetti sauce on the table. She took out some noodles she made earlier. She pulled out a bowl from the cupboard and put a big spoonful of some steaming rice into it. She opened the freezer and grabbed a tub of vanilla ice cream. Mom had gone out of her way to buy and make my favorite foods. In Korean culture, probably every culture, food makes everything better.

"Eat, okay?" she said. "Even if it's just a little."

I took a bite of spaghetti. The deliciousness covered my taste buds, and I savored the flavor of tomatoes and oregano. I didn't gag. I ate slowly. Mom sat with me. She grabbed another bowl and scooped a generous serving of vanilla ice cream into it. She even took out the chocolate syrup and let me put as much as I wanted all over my dessert.

After the accident, I wasn't allowed to run or do anything that might hurt my head. Mom took the doctor's words seriously and decided I shouldn't work at the station. In fact, I was also unable to carry on my duties as the class mascot. I had to give that up, too. I was disappointed, but what could I do?

"Take the year off," Mom told me when I asked her if she needed me to go to the station with her. "Get better so you can help later."

I felt so bad. I didn't want to leave Mom alone at the station working those long hours. I wanted to help. But she stood her ground. That's when Albert stepped up to the plate.

"Don't worry about it," he said to me. "I'll go with Mom. Just heal. Don't be retarded."

I was grateful to my brother for his backhanded show of love and concern. True to his word, he helped Mom for almost every shift that I missed while I "healed." I stayed home and was glad for the time off. I watched a lot of television. I read a ton of books. I did my homework, which oddly felt good because I could do it without worrying about being interrupted every few minutes by a customer. I reveled in the sheer simplicity of my daily routine of going to school, coming home, washing the rice, doing my homework, and going to bed. I had time to process my life and my perspective. I thought about everything that had happened to me and Mom. To my family. From her humble beginnings in Korea to her difficult life as a widow working crazy hours, to that very moment where I was rubbing the scar on my head. I was grateful for all of it. I was alive. If I had died with that kind of hatred in my heart... I finally understood Mom. "Just be nice," and life wouldn't be so hard. She was always strangely at peace with her situation – raising three kids on her own with a business in Compton. She was always nice and she seemed all the better for it. Now it was my turn to "understanding."

During my vacation from the booth, I focused on my studies and on that ridiculously hard A.P. Bio class. I ended up missing the rest of Mr. Hagino's summer prep course because of the accident, but when I started the regular school year in September 1996, I went to his classroom during lunch period. I would have seen him later that day, but I wanted to go talk to him and see about making up the summer course work I'd missed. I opened the green door with the hydraulic stop and saw Mr. Hagino sitting at his desk writing notes on some papers. There were no students. I walked in.

"Hi, Mr. Hagino," I said as I stood in front of him.

He looked up at me.

"Carol," he said. "How are you doing?"

Surprised by his easy tone, I nodded my head at him and said, "Better."

"Good," he said. "Grab a seat and bring it here. Let's talk about what you missed."

As we sat there chatting about the chapters I had to cover over the next three weeks in order to catch up with the rest of my class, he treated me with patience and kindness. I wasn't used to that, especially coming from him. When we finally finished the review, he closed the book and asked me what had happened over the summer. I told him the whole story. He listened quietly.

"I'm glad you're okay," he said.

"Thanks," I said. "Thanks for everything."

"I'll see you later then," he said as he got up.

"Okay."

After that day, Mr. Hagino treated me differently. He didn't kick me out of class, and I genuinely tried to learn. We had found respect for one another. I finally realized he was only trying to teach me my freshman year.

I had been a stubborn ass, and he had no tolerance for stubborn asses in his classroom. That year I studied as hard as I could. When my class took the A.P. Bio test, Mr. Hagino pulled me aside and told me that it would simply be "luck of the draw" on which test I'd get and how well I'd do. If I got a hard test, I'd get a low score. If I got an easier test, I'd scrape by with a three. (The test is based on a one-to-five scale with three as a passing number). When our scores came back I went to see Mr. Hagino during lunch period to tell him the news.

"And?" he asked as I walked in.

"I got a two," I said.

He nodded his head and pursed his lips for a moment as he let the information sink in.

I let out a sigh. "At least I tried," I said.

He smiled and gave me a hug.

"You did your best, sweetie, and that's what counts," he said. "Good job."

For several months after the accident, I stayed away from the gas station and focused on my school work. I felt horrible for not helping, especially as Albert would come home, angry, pissed, and tired. Occasionally, he would tell me what happened at the station; sometimes it was a story about some guy driving off with the pump in his car again, or about some accident or some customer he got in a fight with. It was like looking in a mirror; that was me before the accident.

"Can't I come?" I begged Mom five months after I got out of the hospital. "I'm fine now. I can work. I can help."

"No!" Mom said. "Stay home! Clean the house and rest. The doctor said you need to rest for a long time. Don't ask again!"

Disappointed, I watched her go out the door with Albert as they headed to the station. I had started to miss being in the booth. I know it was a strange thing to miss, but I did. I wasn't sure if it was just people-watching withdrawal, but I justified it by telling myself that being home alone was scary, which it was. The home invasion robbery taught me that even the sanctity of home wasn't impervious to crime and violence. I missed my little world, my safe haven of bulletproof glass and metal countertops, of rock solid walls, and the smell of grease, gas, and commerce.

It wasn't until April 1997, several months later, that I finally went back to the booth. I had convinced Mom that I was in good condition and that being there couldn't possibly hurt me. I said I would take it easy and only work a few hours to help her. She finally agreed.

When I started working again, I had a new perspective. I changed the way I saw people after the accident and the way I viewed life; I accepted it because I was just happy to be alive even if it meant I had to work in that cashier's booth. Besides, one day I'd grow up and leave the station and work wherever I wanted to. So, when I went back to Compton, I stopped being so mean and racist. How could I be? I stopped getting angry when someone called me a gook. After all, being called a racist name was a whole lot better than being stuck in a hospital bed with so many staples in my head that even Frankenstein would have shuddered.

I remembered that it was Asians who had held me and my brothers captive in our home just a few years prior. I realized that everyone is a victim in some form or fashion, no matter the color of our skin or our class in society. I started to see that I shouldn't always take the insults so seriously because there were other things in life that were harder and worse to endure than just racial slurs; things like an acute subdural hematoma and near-death experiences that happened by sheer chance. I learned to let go of my hatred of blacks, Mexicans, and even myself and that bulletproof cashier's booth. I realized I needed to understand and accept all the beautiful facets of my ethnicity, my Korean heritage, and my American-born identity. I finally understood we're all in this together. Making it harder than it already is, just isn't worth it. *Fuck the racism. Fuck the crime. Forget all of it,* I thought. *If God had just given me a second chance at life, I wasn't going to squander it being a racial bigot or an angry bitch.* So, I changed my perspective. We all needed to respect and help each other, see beyond the color and class lines because quite frankly, I almost ended up not being able to see or do anything at all.

Over the years, I learned more about my ethnic roots. I learned that working hard is instilled in Koreans because of our history. I learned that Mom's only choice in life was to work or starve. That's why she never shut the station down voluntarily. She never took vacation, except for one time in the summer of 1997 when the company closed our operations for two weeks so that they could replace the tanks in the ground and renovate the property. The days off presented Mom with a very rare opportunity: she could go visit her family in Korea. Mom planned the trip. She hadn't seen her family in twenty-three years. Grandfather had already passed away, but Grandmother was still alive.

We took a nonstop flight to Korea in late July 1997. I was seventeen years old. We landed at Incheon International Airport, grabbed our luggage, and started to walk around. We looked for the signs my aunts said they would be holding so that we would recognize them. Mom was nervous and excited. I was nervous, too. I was going to Mom's home, to the land of my ethnic roots. I had heard so much about my relatives; they were kind, driven, happy people who never forgot about their sister in America. I was glad that I would be able to meet them and my only living grandparent; my grandmother was in her late sixties or early seventies at the time.

Mom wore new clothes - a gold colored shirt with a small zebra and a few fake jewel studs on the front, and a new pair of black pants. She had dyed her hair to hide the gray and brought thousands of dollars' worth of beef jerky, coffee, clothes, medicine, and other gifts for her family. In Korea, back in the late 1990s, meat, coffee, and medicines were expensive, so Mom made sure to bring enough for all her siblings.

After we walked around the airport for five minutes looking for my aunts, I spotted the signs and pointed toward them, seeing in these women the same features as my mother. Mom rushed over to greet them. They all gathered around her and embraced the prodigal sibling who had finally come home. They commented on how she had changed, how she had aged, how good she looked. There were many tears, and when the commotion finally settled, Mom took a deep breath and told them she wanted to go see their mother.

We drove to Grandmother's house, a small one-story building near my youngest aunt's home. Mom bowed to her mother in respect, love, and honor. She had come home a successful woman with three healthy children. Mom had fulfilled Grandmother's hopes and wishes that she would be well and happy.

"Welcome home," Grandmother said to Mom.

We toured South Korea and visited various places. One of the first spots we went to was her childhood hometown in Kwangju. I saw where she grew up; she wasn't kidding about the little shack she used to tell me about as a kid. I couldn't go in to see it because the land and the house had been sold, but from what I could tell it was tiny. As our trip unfolded, I found out that the stories she had been telling me over the years were all true.

"Your mother used to walk to those mountains over there," my fifth aunt said as she pointed in the distance to twin peaks about two miles away from their childhood home. "She picked wild melons for us. She used to eat some there so she wouldn't be hungry and then she'd bring some back for us."

I stared at my fifth aunt, flabbergasted. I looked for Mom who was standing a few feet away, her arm looped in my grandmother's.

"Mom, you really did walk two miles to pick melons?!"

"Why would I lie about something like that?"

"It's just that, you know, parents always tell their kids crazy stories like that just to make them feel like they have it good."

"Yes, your mother used to help so much," Grandmother said. "She took care of your aunts and your uncles, she is a good daughter."

My mom looked down at the dirt, but I could see that she was happy. I was glad for her because it was obvious that Grandmother was proud of her. Grandma was spry, and I could have easily mistaken her for being fifty. She had curly black hair, and it was clear that in terms of appearance, Mom didn't take after her. I wanted to get to know Grandmother and hoped we could talk, but I knew before we could get the chance, I had to show her deference in the traditional Korean way. So, I bought her a gift of candies to eat from a roadside vendor, walked her to her house after our sojourn to the countryside was over, and offered to help her with whatever she needed.

When we got there, Grandmother asked me to move some plants and put them on the table. As I did little chores for her, she chatted about how she loved farming and how she used to grow rice and vegetables when she lived on the farm with Grandfather and Mom. She told me how hard they had to work. She and Grandfather were born during the long Japanese occupation of Korea, which stretched from 1910 to 1945. The Japanese had already begun to occupy the Korean peninsula during the Russo-Japanese War in the early 1900s and had virtually taken over the country by 1905, after the signing of the Japan-Korea Protection Treaty.

Grandmother, who had lived most of her girlhood during the latter half of the occupation, told me stories of that time, when Koreans still wore mostly *hanbok*, which is traditional Korean dress, and how she had to cook and clean and help the family. She talked about how precious food and education were and told me she had little opportunity to pursue academic ambitions or any ambitions for that matter because she was expected to leave her family, get married, have children, and support her husband at home by being the dutiful Korean wife. Then she stopped talking for a moment and gave me an intent look.

"Are you going to go to college?" she asked as I opened the bag of candy I bought her and handed her a piece.

"Yes," I answered.

"You must go to school so you can find a good job and work and make money."

"I will," I promised.

"For me and your mother, things were difficult. Food was hard to find, and your grandfather and I didn't have enough money to buy the things we needed like clothes," she continued. "Once, when your mom was young, I had to make new soles for her shoes from rice leaves. Your mother did not complain."

I nodded my head in understanding.

"For many years, we worked hard," she reiterated. "When they rang the bell in the morning, I was already up and working and getting everyone ready for school and then working on the farm. It was a different life."

"You must have suffered a lot," I said to show my respect and understanding.

"No, I didn't suffer. I did what I needed to do, that's all. Everyone does what needs to be done, and this is not suffering," she said softly.

As she finished her sentence, I picked up a photo of my grandfather from one of the tables in the living room. We were sitting on bamboo mats she had rolled out for us. I could see that all my uncles and aunts as well as my mom took after him, with a strong jawline, big nose, and prominent eyes. He had passed away years before our visit to Korea. I was disappointed that I would never meet him. He had a look of determination and fire that I wished I could have witnessed when he was alive. The picture was the one thing that made me regret not being born and raised in Korea.

"What was Grandfather like?" I asked as I ran a finger over a different picture, this one of Grandfather in his old age.

"He was strong and he worked hard."

"Is my mom like him?" I ventured.

She smiled.

"She looks like him," she said as she took his picture from me. "They all do. But your mom, she was the only one who left. I worried for your mother. I have not seen her for many years, and I'm glad she came home so that I could see that she is happy."

"Mom is one of the strongest, most persevering people I know. Did she get that from you?"

"I don't know," she said, smiling. "Maybe she did, or maybe she always had it in her."

Then she went quiet for a few moments.

"Your mom was born in the Year of the Dragon," she finally said. "She is the only one who could have left Korea."

I had always thought Mom was born in the Year of the Rabbit, 1951. She later told me that when she came to the States, they mistakenly put her year of birth one year too early. This is because Asians count their age starting from conception. So, Mom told the American official her age and he counted backwards to 1951. However, Mom was born in 1952. Learning that she was a dragon explained a lot of things about Mom. Dragons are dominant, ambitious, and driven, unafraid of challenges and taking risks. They're also passionate and live by their own rules. If left on their own, they are successful. After Dad died, she was alone. Dragons also rarely ask for help but often help others and can have tempers that flare quickly. They also like to lead rather than be led. It was no surprise to me when I found all this out later in life. It just made sense because my mom ran the gas station on her own and never remarried.

"Mom is like you," I said again to grandma.

She smiled and handed me a piece of candy.

Mom at the gas station in 2012 being interviewed for a documentary. Photo by Keun-pyo "Root" Park.

Today, I am proud of Mom and her success, which is measured not by the amount of money she makes, but by the sheer simplicity of her joy in being able to eat three square meals a day and sleep in a comfortable bed. I finally understood that the work Mom and I did together created a bond between us that made me a stronger person, able to endure that which life has offered me. She has taught me how to survive. She has taught me that my Korean face should not stop me from being who or what I want to be, but that it should enhance my experiences in life and make me a better person. I am Korean American after all.

I am not bitter or angry with her about anything. I'm indebted to her for instilling in me a drive to succeed and survive, even if she did tell me I was old enough to work because I was double digits. I learned that there is beauty in simple things like a ten-minute break in a forty-eight-hour shift, in being able to spend time with Mom even if it is in a cashier's booth, and in simply being able to live at all. If I hadn't learned about racism or hadn't been called a gook or chink, I would have never tried to understand or find out about my Korean heritage. I would have never found my Korean American identity. The accident gave me a wakeup call the LA Riots didn't. The robbery didn't either, nor did the shooting. But that's because the road I was on was paved in obstacles and like Dorothy in the *Wizard of Oz*, I had to find my courage, my brain, and my heart.

"How are you?" one of the regulars asked when I started working again. "I haven't seen you in ages!"

I handed the woman, a teacher at one of the schools, her usual two boxes of menthol cigarettes. She dropped the money in the tray and pushed her blonde braids out of her face.

"Well, I just took a break for a while," I said as I got her change. "But it's nice to be back."

Mom and I chatting in the garage at the gas station
in 2012. Photo by Keun-pyo "Root" Park.

Epilogue

Mom finally hired someone to take over weekend shifts in 2006. My brothers and I had graduated from college, and times had changed. I had been working as a cashier and as a business reporter for one of the local papers for years at this point. Mom was getting older, tired, and less capable of working those marathon hours, and she could see how tired I was getting. When she finally hired the new worker, I happily trained him, but this meant I was no longer a cashier. I was twenty-six years old. I didn't know what to do with myself. So, I spent my weekends at Mom's house offering to do chores; clean the kitchen, do laundry, vacuum, you name it. I was so used to working at the station that the boatload of free time I had was disturbing.

I ended up thinking about everything that we had been through. I thought about the craziness, the lessons, and how at the end of the day, what I learned from working at the station and from Mom was how to survive. Mom instilled in me the determination to accomplish my goals. But, when people ask me if I could change the way I grew up, I say: "Abso-fucking-lutely." Who wouldn't? But the facts are facts, and I begrudgingly admit that if I hadn't gone through what I did, I wouldn't be where I am today.

Months after Mom hired the new worker, I found myself wondering about the station and my cashier's booth. Was the pimp still around? How about that teacher? Was Eggo still looking out for us even though we weren't there as much? I was strangely curious about my old stomping grounds. I wanted to sit on that blue cushioned chair and see if it still felt the same. Finally, I caved and asked Mom if I could go with her to Compton one Saturday afternoon.

"How's everything at the station?" I asked her.

It had been more than six months since I had been back to help out. I wanted to see the booth, see what we were selling, see if we were keeping up with the gum quota I had set so many years prior.

"Okay," she said.

"How's Eggo?"

"Fine."

How I hated her short, definite answers.

"Do you need me to go with you to the station today?" I asked.

"No," Mom said.

"Are you sure?"

"Yes."

"But, you need help stocking the cigarettes and the soda."

I gave Mom a pathetic look. She stood her ground. She's always been hard to persuade.

"No, there's no reason for you to come," she said.

"It's been a long time since I've been to the station with you," I said. "Besides, Albert's sick today, and you need the help. How are you going to lift all those boxes and stock everything and still make it back to go to the bank in time?"

Mom gave me a stern look, but my reasoning was sound. She shrugged her shoulders. I followed her to the car. We drove to the gas station together, like days of old, only it was broad daylight, and I wasn't grouchy from being woken up so early in the morning. After the short ride, we pulled into the station. Out of habit, I looked around to make sure the area was safe. I glanced toward the bus bench, the garage, the pumps; it was all the same. I rubbed my sweaty palms together.

The mechanic was working on a car. Graffiti still decorated our walls and signs. There was Eggo, sitting on the white plastic chair near the glass door leading into the mechanic's bay. I clenched my fists and got out of the car, readying myself for a day at work. My muscles tensed at the familiar sight of cars and people and the busy intersection. I straightened out my long-sleeved black shirt and jeans; I wasn't wearing my uniform today. We walked toward the cashier's booth and I nodded at a couple of familiar customers. After that day, I stopped working as a cashier for good. I only visited to drop off inventory or fill up on gas. Finally, that bulletproof chapter of my life was over.

As the years passed by, I thought about the LA Riots and why the violence happened. Research and studies always point to the same reasons: police brutality, racism, government neglect, and poverty. When 2012 rolled around and the community observed the twentieth anniversary of the LA Riots, the question that was and is on all of our minds – Mom's, my brothers', Eggo's, mine, and the community's – is, Will and can something like the LA Riots happen again?

"Yes," says University of California Riverside's Professor of Ethnic Studies Edward T. Chang. "All the structural conditions that existed back then still exist today. If you don't address the structural conditions that ignited the race riots, whether another riot happens again isn't the question. Rather, the question is where and when it will."[37]

And it did happen again, this time in Ferguson, St. Louis, Missouri, after the fatal shooting of eighteen-year-old African American Michael Brown by a white police officer on August 8, 2014. On August 9, 2014, people in Ferguson took to the streets. Rioting occurred. For several weeks people rioted, looted, and protested. I watched the news with dismay. Professor Chang's words rang through my mind as images of clashing police and civilians paraded across my television screen.

When Mom heard the news of the rioting in Ferguson, she shook her head and muttered a grateful prayer that it wasn't happening in Los Angeles. But that didn't mean it wouldn't happen again in another city. And sure enough, it did. On April 12, 2015, Freddie Gray, a twenty-five-year-old African American living in Baltimore, was arrested and allegedly injured by police. Protests began on April 18 while Gray was hospitalized. He died on April 19. More protests, rioting, and looting followed. For weeks Baltimore's residents found themselves submerged in violence. Protesters demanded justice – so reminiscent of the Rodney King case and subsequent riots – community leaders and activists demanded that the government do something about police brutality and racism against African Americans.

As the rioting dragged on, the Maryland Army National Guard was called in as a state of emergency was declared in Baltimore. The riots lasted for weeks, but when order was finally restored and protests simmered down to peaceful demonstrations, Mom and I were left wondering, once again, could this happen in Los Angeles?

Maybe. The difference today is that the demographics of Los Angeles have changed since the 1980s and 1990s. More Southeast Asians, Arab Americans, and Hispanics have taken over businesses and moved into inner cities. The Black-Korean Conflict has simmered down. The African American population has decreased in Los Angeles County in what has been called "black flight." African Americans left the beleaguered cities of Los Angeles and moved to places like Rialto, San Bernardino, and other Inland Southern California cities.

Myself? I moved to the Inland Empire. In that Inland region – which is about sixty miles away from LA – I'm satisfied with my slow pace of life, my job, the diversity without as much racial tension. When I think about the riots, I think about how my life has been shaped by the uprising and the home invasion robbery. The riots made me choose a different direction in life by making me realize, Korean Americans and really, minorities in general, need a voice.

Over the years, Mom's health began to fail. She tried to hold on to the station for as long as she could, but as diabetes took its toll on her once-strong body and her kidneys failed, she had to sell. The three-hour dialysis sessions were too much to handle for her to work at the same time. Albert took over the station for her until finally she found a buyer. Mom looked back at her life and all the things she went through at the station and settled for the fact that the business had fed her family, sent her children to school, and that we were happy and successful. Even after we finally sold the station, Mom believes it was all worth it.

On December 5, 2014, Mom and Albert officially relinquished the station to its new owners; they were a former Egyptian worker and his family members. We were finally free. That day, I went with my brother to the station to hand over the keys. Mom didn't go because she had dialysis treatment that day. As my brother and I drove to the station, we reminisced about the small things, the rough things, and the freedom and relief we felt over finally, *finally*, selling the station. We never had to worry about bullets, gangs, and violence while working in a cashier's booth again. I rubbed my hands together in preparation for the final walk-through when Albert parked the car. It was a cool afternoon and clouds dimmed the light of the sun.

"You hungry?" Albert asked me as we walked into the garage bay. "Want to get some tacos one last time?"

I laughed and nodded my head in agreement. I ran across the street. The complex still housed the donut shop. The market was still there. The 99 cents store was still there. But, the Chinese food place was no longer there and was now a Mexican eatery called *Viva Jalisco*, which was formerly the *Jugos Tropicales* on Rosecrans. I greeted the owner. We'd known each other for years. I used to run over during a break in my shift on warm afternoons and get burritos and enchiladas for me and Mom.

146

She gave me a warm smile. "You're back," she said. "You've been closed for a few days, huh?"

Albert had shut operations at the station down for several days in preparation for the takeover.

"Yup," I said. "But we don't own the station anymore, we sold it."

"Wow! After all these years! How is your Mom?" she asked.

"She's tired," I said. "But we're happy."

"Congratulations," she said. "Come back anytime! Have some tacos!"

I proceeded to order some enchiladas, tacos, and two horchatas.

"Here you go," the owner said. "Enjoy."

"Thank you," I said. "It's been wonderful eating your food, and I wish you continued success."

She came from behind the register and patted me on the back. "It's been good knowing you for so long," she said. "Take care. Tell your mom goodbye for me." Food in hand, I walked out of the restaurant and headed back to the station. As I made my way across the street I looked at the station and wondered if it would still be there five years from now. But what did I care anymore? We sold it! Albert and I ate our food in the garage. He looked excited. His eyes were gleaming, something I hadn't seen in a long time; probably since he had taken over the business for Mom.

"That's it!" he said. "No more of this crappy station!"

As we waited for the new owners to come, I looked around and took some photos with my phone. I looked at the remnants of the once bustling mechanic's shop. Boxes of oil and antifreeze were stacked in the middle of the garage. I thought about all the times we had spent there and all the things we'd experienced: when Dad caught a thief trying to steal his tools, or the time when there was a robbery and we had to hide under the tables in the office, or when I accidently crashed Mom's car into the pumps while trying to learn to drive. I took another photo and ate the rest of my food. After we finished lunch, Albert and I went into the booth. One of the workers was there, getting things ready for the new owners. I greeted him with a huge grin.

"Faiz!" I said. "This is it!"

He smiled and asked if we could take some pictures with him. I agreed. As we snapped a few shots with his camera phone and mine, the new owners showed up. They walked around the station and looked in the garage as Albert explained to them what each key was for, what was left for them in terms of inventory, and how the computer worked. When the uncles of the former worker arrived, I shook their hands and thanked them for purchasing the station.

"No, no, thank you for this opportunity and allowing us to buy it," they said. "Tell your mom this is still her place and she is welcome anytime!"

I appreciated the gesture and expressed my thanks to him. As Albert walked around the station with one of the new owners, I went out and took down the yellow caution tape that had roped off the exits and entrances to the station. I took out my pocket knife and cut the tape off the pumps and air machine. Faiz came outside to help as everything got set up for the opening of a new shift with the new owners.

After a few minutes, two cars pulled in, and I watched as the new owners made their first sales. The customers walked back to their cars to pump their gas. One of them had trouble with the pump. I walked over to help him. The older black man had on a nice bowler hat and tan slacks.

"Hello, sir," I said as I walked up to him. "Let me help you with that."

I jiggled the handle of pump number 2, remembering how it liked to catch now and then. I waved at Faiz who had returned to the booth and gestured for him to turn on the pump again. I pressed the 87-grade button and stuck the nozzle into the man's car.

"There you go," I said as I squeezed the handle. "Have a great day."

"Thanks," he said as I walked away. "You too."

My last day at the station; it was a cloudy,
gloomy day. (Photo from family archives).

Sometimes, out of habit or nostalgia, I visit the gas station. Even after
Mom sold it, I still go and look at the place. When I go there, I still see
some of the same people, the same teachers, workers, mothers, and fathers
that haven't left the area. I also see the growing Hispanic population and
the new Arab American businessmen that are buying up tobacco shops
and gas stations. I see the changes, like the influx of new ethnic minorities,
like Southeast Asians, that have nothing to do with preventing another
riot. I see changes that are ingredients for another civil unrest, uprising,
or whatever you want to call it. Even though the racial tension between
blacks and Koreans has died down, those structural conditions Professor
Chang talked about still exist.

Today, the Black-Korean Conflict is no longer at the forefront of the
media's attention. This isn't because we opened dialogue and decided to
all "get along" but rather because Koreans don't own as many businesses
in inner cities, though they still operate shops in other areas. Today,
businesses in inner cities are run by a mix of ethnicities including Southeast
Asians, Arab Americans, and Mexican Americans.

Racial tension still simmers. The only thing that has really changed
are the players. During the twentieth anniversary of the LA Riots in 2012,

many people talked about the racism that continues to this day. Whether it's between blacks and Koreans, Mexicans and blacks, or whomever, racism and unrest still brews in our inner cities all over the nation. Poverty is still a problem. The gap between the haves and the have-nots is still wide. Government neglect is still an issue. Police brutality is still a problem—just look at what happened in Ferguson. Just think about the Black Lives Matter movement.

Another thing of significance that happened in the year of the twentieth anniversary of the LA Riots was the death of Rodney King. He was "in a state of drug and alcohol-induced delirium" and was found deceased in a pool at his Rialto, California home on June 17, 2012.[38] He was forty-seven. The news of his death brought back memories of the LA Riots and the unrest of the early 1990s; it made me think about the Korean community, my mother, and how we managed to survive the chaos of those tumultuous years.

"How do you feel about all of this, Mom?" I asked as we followed coverage of King's death.

"Why?" Mom asked.

"Don't you have any hard feelings about what happened? All that trouble? The looting? The worries? The racism? Anything? I know I do!"

"It was difficult," Mom said.

"You know, working all those years was really tough for me," I said. "The racism and crime was terrible."

"I'm just glad we're all okay," Mom said. "That's all in the past. Don't bother yourself with things like that. Worry about your future."

The problem was that I did worry. When Rodney King died his words resonated in my mind: "Can we all get along?"

Bend in the Road

Even though Mom is very ill, she's still fighting strong. She's been on dialysis for a few years now. She tries to keep her spirits up. She still jokes with me and treats me like I'm twelve. Once, while she was in the hospital being monitored for her heart in 2012 she said this:

"Hurry up and get married. I want grandchildren. If you don't hurry up soon, all your good eggs will shrivel up and you will have stupid children."

I laughed so hard that the nurse had to tell me to keep it down, there were other patients sleeping.

"I didn't work that hard so you could be barren," Mom continued. "Hurry up!"

What could I say? Her hard work and those crazy graveyard shifts helped put me and my brothers through school. Mom worked hard because she knew that the only way to have a better life than what she had was through education. She worked hard to save enough money to send us to college. I did my best to make her proud. Today, I wonder about our future. I worry that riots will keep happening because we just don't know how to "get along." So, what can we do? While awareness is the start, it's not action. We need action to create change like the Black Lives Matter movement. We need to work together to find the solution. That will be a long, hard road, but we must take the first step.

What I've learned since 1992 is that it's not up to the government or one single person to stop the violence or to stop history from repeating itself. It's up to all of us – it's in our hands.

Endnotes

1   U.S. Census Bureau. "Table B02006: Asian Alone by Selected Groups. Universe: Total Asian Alone Population." 2016. U.S. Census Bureau. United States 2010-2014 American Community Survey 5-Year Estimates. http://factfinder.census.gov/faces/tableservices/jsf/pages/productview. xhtml?pid=ACS_14_5YR_B02006&prodType=table.

2   Marbella, J. (2015, June 13). Korean-American merchants face hurdles in rebuilding after Baltimore riot. Retrieved from *The Baltimore Sun*. http://www. baltimoresun.com/business/bs-md-korean-stores-freddie-gray-20150613-story. html

3   Audi, T. and Emshwiller, J. R. (2012, April 27). Attitudes toward police and race relations have turned positive since devastating riots; economy is big concern now. Retrieved from *The Wall Street Journal*. http://www.wsj.com

4   Chang, Edward T. "New Urban Crisis: Korean-African American Relations." *Koreans in the Hood: Conflict with African Americans*, edited by Kwang Chung Kim, Johns Hopkins University Press, 1999, pp. 39-59.

5   Sides, Josh. "Straight into Compton: American Dreams, Urban Nightmares, and the Metamorphosis of a Black Suburb." American Quarterly. Volume 56, Number 3, September 2004. Pg. 583-605. Johns Hopkins University Press.

6   Min, Pyong Gap. "Koreans' Immigration to the U.S. History and Contemporary Trends." Queens College and the Graduate Center of CUNY, The Research Center for Korean Community, Queens College of CUNY, Research Report No. 3, January 2011.

7   According to K.W. Lee, the godfather of Asian American Journalism and former publisher/editor of the *Korea Times* English edition, American media stirred the pot of racial tension and pitted blacks and Koreans against one another in news coverage.

8   II Maugh. T. H. (1995, June 30). Bullets Fired at Sky Cited in 38 Deaths: Study: Hospital lists holiday data over seven years. Police question it. *The Los Angeles Times*. Retrieved from: http://articles.latimes.com/1995-06-30/local/ me-18804_1_gunshot-wounds

9   Queally, J. (2015, July 29). Watts Riots: Traffic stop was the spark that ignited days of destruction in L.A. *The LA Times*. Retrieved from http://www.latimes. com/local/lanow/la-me-ln-watts-riots-explainer-20150715-htmlstory.html.

10 Reinhold, R. (1991, July 10). Violence and racism are routine in Los Angeles, police study says. *The New York Times*. Retrieved from https://www.nytimes. com/books/98/02/08/home/rodney-report.html

11 Adams, C. (2016, March 3). March 3, 1991: Rodney King beating caught on video. *CBS News*. Retrieved from http://www.cbsnews.com/news/march-3ʳᵈ-199 1-rodney-king-lapd-beating-caught-on-video/

12 Jennings, A. (2016, March 16). 25 years later, vigil marks Latasha Harlins' death, which fed anger during Rodney King riots. *The LA Times*. Retrieved from http:// www.latimes.com/local/california/la-me-0317-latasha-harlins-vigil-20160317-story.html.

13 Unites States Department of Labor, Bureau of Labor Statistics. "Labor Force Statistics from the Current Population Survey." http://data.bls.gov/timeseries/ LNU04000000?years_option=all_years&periods_option=specific_ periods&periods=Annual+Data.

14 Chang, Edward. "Building Minority Coalitions: A Case Study of Korean and African Americans." *Korea Journal of Population and Development*, Volume 21, Number 1, July 1992, pp. 37-56.

15 Martin, H. (1991, October 30). "Korean Shopkeeper Killed in Robbery: Violence: In another incident, a Korean-owned-liquor store is burned, but community leaders say the episodes do not seem racially motivated." Retrieved from *The Los Angeles Times*. *http://articles.latimes.com/1991-10-30/local/ me-709_1_korean-american-community*.

16 Chung, Angie Y. *Legacies of Struggle: Conflict and Cooperation in Korean American Politics*. Stanford University Press. 2007.

17 Various media outlets reported on the incident including major publications.

18 Mydans, S. (1992, April 30). Los Angeles Policemen Acquitted in Taped Beating. *The New York Times*. Retrieved from http://www.nytimes.com/learning/general/ onthisday/big/0429.html.

19 Ibid

20 Ibid

21 Ibid

22 Staff. (2016, April 28). The L.A. Riots 24 Years Later. *The Los Angeles Times*. Retrieved from http://timelines.latimes.com/los-angeles-riots/.

23 Ibid

24 Staff. (5, April 2012). Deaths During the L.A. riots. *The Los Angeles Times*. Retrieved from http://spreadsheets.latimes.com/la-riots-deaths/

25 Retired Major General James D. Delk stated this information in an article for the California State Military Department/The California Military Museum.

26 Mydans, S. (1992, April 30). Los Angeles Policemen Acquitted in Taped Beating. *The New York Times*. Retrieved from http://www.nytimes.com/learning/general/onthisday/big/0429.html.

27 Yi, Eugene. SAIGU: AN ORAL HISORY. *KoreAm Journal*. April 2012.

28 Ibid

29 Ibid

30 Staff. (2016, April 28). The L.A. Riots 24 Years Later. *The Los Angeles Times*. Retrieved from http://timelines.latimes.com/los-angeles-riots/.

31 Ibid

32 Ibid

33 Ibid

34 Audi, T. and Emshwiller, J. R. (2012, April 27). Attitudes toward police and race relations have turned positive since devastating riots; economy is big concern now. Retrieved from *The Wall Street Journal*. http://www.wsj.com.

35 Hunt, Darnell. "American Toxicity: Twenty Years After the 1992 Los Angeles 'Riots'." *Ameriasia Journal*. Volume 38, Issue 1, 2012, pp. ix-xviii.

36 Staff. (5, April 2012). Deaths During the L.A. riots. *The Los Angeles Times*. Retrieved from http://spreadsheets.latimes.com/la-riots-deaths/

37 Prof. Edward T. Chang has spoken on this topic since 1992 and in several conversations with me throughout the last several years.

38 Wilson, S. and Duke, A. (2012, August 23). Police: Rodney King's accidental drowning involved drugs. *CNN.com*. Retrieved from http://www.cnn.com/2012/08/23/us/rodney-king-autopsy/.

About the Author

Carol Park is a researcher, filmmaker, and award-winning journalist. She holds a master of fine arts degree in creative writing from UC Riverside and is a Korean American studies expert. She wrote and produced the documentary *The 1992 Los Angeles Riots: Reflections on Our Future (2012)*. She has written for magazines, newspapers, and journals and won several awards from the Society of Professional Journalists. Her articles have appeared in numerous publications. She currently lives in Riverside, California.

Made in the USA
San Bernardino, CA
02 April 2019